MINE'S BIGGER THAN YOURS

By Steve Hance

Marion, Ia 52302

Library of Congress Number
95-095341

ISBN Number 0-9111119-69-8

Preface

"The sun comes up as the birds begin to sing
The flowers start to bloom in the middle of the spring.
The day goes on as you learn from a friend,
It's nice to know there is always someone you can depend on.
There's a beautiful world that you can help."

By Alison Hance

It's a simple thought, yet it encompasses many values and ideals. It's a simple description of life by my ten year old daughter. We were all born with this simplicity but it dies as we become educated and socialized. The ability to understand the needs of others, to feel the joy of new experiences and the capacity to recognize the basic values of life and living become distorted as we mature and become more materialistic.

The socialization and aging processes used to be simple. Even today, simplicity can still be found in many of America's small towns. When I return to the small farming community where I grew up, the simple life still exists. People walk along the streets and speak to one another. A handshake is worth more than any attorney's contract. When someone is in need, everyone comes to help. It takes far less money to live in this rural environment, and the destructive behaviors that are common in most cities and corporations aren't tolerated.

As you look around, you discover that the world is a rapidly changing place. This is not all bad. But the manner in which change occurs determines whether the effect on human beings is positive or negative. Throughout the country there are increases in chronic disease. Stress-related illnesses and behavior are appearing more and more often. Nearly 80% of the diseases that doctors treat are now stress-related. Social injustice has become the norm and our legal system is overloaded with decisions that reinforce social injustice.

Society encourages us to focus on the individual not on society, not on what is good for the environment just on "me." If it doesn't affect me, it's unimportant. If it does affect me, it must turn out my way regardless of the negative impact on others.

Why did I decide to write this book? It's simple. After 23 years of climbing the corporate ladder to a vice-presidential office, I found that life was empty. After 23 years of dealing with both management and hourly employees, I found that I was not alone. Most people are immensely frustrated. The organizations they work for have abandoned most of the basic values our society was founded upon. Trust, compassion and integrity are just words in the dictionary. They've lost any real meaning in our daily lives. Theft, violent crime, divorce, gangs, and legal exploits are their replacements.

You may be surprised to know that writing this book was the best experience that I've had in the last 23 years. I discovered that I had lost touch with the basic values in my life. My wife and children had become strangers and now I am beginning to know them again. The world actually became brighter each day. As I found myself developing and growing I could see pain all around me caused by manipulation in the business world, and I saw the disastrous effects of corporate games on society and individuals. Business is not inherently bad, but the core of its structure has become unbalanced. And it is up to business leaders to bring social values and balance back into the millions of lives that are being affected.

Change must occur. We have become a fear-based society of victims looking for someone to blame. People are becoming lifeless in their daily routines and environment with silent screams of anguish that are never heard. Apathy and a loss of trust have swept through the public. Voter turnout is low. Commitment to employers is an obscured memory. Family and the responsibility of parenting have given way to divorce and daycare. Care and concern for the environment have become superficial politics. Religion has become a ritual for many and the belief in a great spirit (by any name) is at an all time low. We have traded our dignity and integrity for personal material gain at the cost of the earth and other human beings.

We have the power of choice to regain a balance through positive changes. And it can begin with one person. As people change, the community changes. Then the workplaces change. Then society changes. The process begins within an individual and spreads. That's how we arrived here and that is how we must return.

Table of Contents

Introduction

The change process driving today's organizations is a force with significant impact on people in their daily lives. Organizations have been striving for decades to reach the pinnacle of perfection. The results that are measured are impressive in many instances. However, there are other outcomes that are not being recognized.

Many of the processes used to drive change are not new ideas, but rather the repackaging of concepts and past ideas, being tried one more time. Marketers can always add one new twist to old material and reintroduce it as a new concept. There are testimonies to the new results, but rarely is there any analysis differentiating superficial from authentic results.

Organizations have been lured into *management-by-best-seller* and *flavor-of-the-month* cycles. These concepts may be somewhat effective for a period of time. But even with all the "new" tools that have been (re)introduced over the last decade, the essence of high performance in any field eludes most organizations.

Before I embarked on this journey, I focused extensive effort on trying to understand why people and organizations were not achieving success. Why does it seem that so many of the programs are failing? The media continuously reports business success stories, and yet statistics indicate that more than 20% of the workforce has endured significant, uncomfortable job changes.

We are in the midst of a quiet but rapid evolution. Some may even describe the change as a revolution. The change, however, is in people not systems. We have become so system focused that the changes in individual and societal values have not been properly valued in today's business equation. Personal honesty and integrity have been rediscovered and are becoming powerful new measurement tools. An awareness of the need for compassion, spirituality, self-esteem and personal satisfaction is reaching levels unseen in recent history.

These personal, individual changes coupled with the appropriate systems have the potential of creating high performance organizations driven by satisfied, creative, productive individuals. In these organizations, employees lead the way, and managers become process guides and observers for the organization.

Structure of This Book

This book has been structured in a format that describes the flow of the quiet revolution. The intent is to examine—

- The status of today's achievements
- The processes currently being used
- The identification of systemic problems
- The process of beginning authentic change

This book is not just for top managers. This information is for all employees regardless of their position, the size or type of their organization, and the degree to which they believe they can initiate change.

As individuals we do have total power. We have the power of choice. We have the power to set examples. We have the power to determine the course and outcome of our lives. We also have the power to reach professional heights and personal happiness that we previously thought were unattainable.

You will recognize yourself and others in this current day drama as you begin to understand where the real power of change is born. You will begin an internal process that will in some way affect how you live your life beyond today.

This book is divided into four sections. The first is very brief and outlines the concepts that are reinforced in us every day-the benefits (we are told) we are reaping from the new age of business. This section also includes a brief accounting of the popular management programs being used today, what they are intended to accomplish, and the outcomes that normally result. The second section identifies real barriers to positive change and shows you how to recognize them. Section 3 is dedicated to the creation of high performance organizations, and the refinement of the popular systems into a format that will work in both personal and professional settings. Section 4 puts it all together, and helps you visualize the results you can anticipate from the cumulative effect of this book's recommendations.

Though you may be taken back by some of the observations in

this book, try to approach the information with an open mind. If you keep your thought processes objective, there is much to gain from these perspectives. Due to the sequential nature of the material I have been advising readers not to skip sections or read ahead.

To your power, peace and happiness.

SECTION 1

We've Come To Where We Deserve to Be

How different are the perceptions?

MANAGEMENT	EMPLOYEES
Zero Defects	Heart Attacks
Productivity	Unemployment
Outsourcing	Loss of Security
Efficiency	Early Retirement
World Markets	Trade Deficits
Intellectual Capital	Lack of Confidence
Financial Performance	Financial Ruin
High Returns	High Blood Pressure
Value Added	Values Destroyed
Breaking Barriers	Broken Families
Personal Gains	Social Losses

What do we believe has really been achieved?

We've all heard the buzz words and phrases used every day in the business environment. And we have all developed our own perception of what these buzz words may mean to us personally. One thing is consistent; most people I've talked with will admit that all the new programs are a band-aid approach and do not deal with the real issues. When you ask someone to outline without using any flavor-of-the-month programs how they bring balance into their personal lives, you get a blank stare. When you ask how an organization can be improved without a best seller approach you get a vacant look. This is frightening because it indicates people are losing their capacity to care.

I was recently appalled as I read a brochure on a management seminar that was going to be offered in a large nearby city. Although I won't mention the name of the organization or quote the specific topics addressed, the brochure essentially stated that employee rights are now out of control. It talked about strategies for withholding management perks from workers, getting rid of pregnant workers legally, how to avoid honoring oral commitments to employees, and how to ensure that employees know who the boss is, just to name a few. Executives are attending these programs to learn what? It is not surprising why employees feel the hopelessness and bitterness that carries over into their personal lives.

I've learned and watched carefully as I moved up the organizational ladder over 23 years. And unfortunately, until my abrupt awakening I became entrapped in the game. The higher individuals move within an organization, the more entitlement they believe they should have. It's driven by greed, ego, and an unquenchable thirst for power and material possessions. The higher they climb, the more they have to lose, so they become part of the good old boy network. The network rarely understands what is reality within the organization. But those in the network clearly understand what is required to stay in it. Company cars, club memberships, stock options, bonuses, special flexible rules-it's all part of playing the game. As I was once told, "...to receive corporate rewards, full compliance is required." This is the point at which they find they are working and living up to others' expectations and level of ethics rather than their own. Their personal identity is gone and they begin to mindlessly espouse the buzz words and try all the new best seller techniques to stay in the network.

I am not criticizing all managers, because not all organizations are run like this. But this dilemma clearly exists in companies, politics, school systems, communities and elsewhere.

There are many popular management tools being used today. Each of these is sold as a program that will improve various functions within the organization such as productivity, profits, employee morale, customer relationships, self-directed work teams, and so on. The list is almost endless.

Under closer scrutiny, many of these programs differ only in the name of the organization that is marketing the information. All promise to enlighten management and demonstrate how to implement the process into their organization. Few if any are offered with a performance guarantee, or on the basis of a percentage of the measurable improvements. Management is just expected to pay for the service outright. I would suggest that if the programs are really effective, more of them would be offered with a guarantee. Few if any consulting firms will consider anything but flat fee compensation.

Following is a summary of some programs that have been popular among management, and a brief look at why these programs have not performed as promised. You may recognize some of the fads that were expected to be the new energy in your organization.

Becoming World Class

American media praises the tremendous strides being made in the world of business. The picture is positive because the factors traditionally used to measure business progress are in fact improving. The measurements that are commonly used do not lie, so the picture that the public is viewing is positive in nature.

Growth and expansion into foreign markets appear as goals in nearly every business plan today. Becoming *world class* is an objective that is appearing over and over. This phrase pops up frequently in speeches and print media, and company newsletters try to explain it to the employees. It's the new pinnacle of success. The concept is a sound strategy to follow and certainly wins the praise of stockholders and Wall Street analysts.

Our economy is based on world markets. You can't go into any shopping center today without finding goods that have been influenced in some way by foreign competition. The clothes we buy, the food we eat, the shoes we wear, the electronic equipment we use have all been transformed due to world markets. The cars we drive and the individual components within those cars have been dramatically influenced by world markets.

The point is not to belabor the effects of the global economy. We have all felt it and we are all participating in it. But, is it new? Weren't there goods from foreign markets entering the U.S. in 1776? Weren't there some countries who did a better job than others in importing and exporting products and services? It's just in recent times since we've become so concerned about the financial impact on our local economy and the continuing trade deficits that the phrase "world class" has taken on such a powerful meaning.

Becoming the Best

We have demonstrated that our country's ingenuity can't be beaten when we are focused on a common goal. A decline in creativity, focus and innovation has also been demonstrated to have disastrous endings. Today there is a solid foundation upon which to build our future. Countries are cooperating to perform under uniform guidelines. We have a long way to go but look at the changes that have occurred already. Environmentally the world has started down a path of sustainable development. The International Standards Organization has developed numerous guidelines, but the introduction of ISO 9000 and ISO 14000 have the potential of creating a level playing field in the areas of quality and environmental, health and safety. The European markets are opening up as never before and the Pacific Rim offers opportunities for every business.

International joint ventures, strategic alliances, marketing agreements and distribution arrangements are blazing new territories that benefit organizations, people, the global economy and standards of living. These benefits don't happen overnight but rather are a gradual process that goes through a learning and growing period until it becomes an integral part of the global economic system.

The point is simple. A global economy is the reality in which we must function. But this is really not new. The rules of the game are beginning to clearly emerge and many of the processes and certification standards have been in dormant existence for 50 years. We are just learning to recognize, learn and use these systems. Complete conformance does not guarantee success as so many companies have discovered.

The Age of Knowledge

We now hear about our *intellectual capital* and the *age of knowledge.* Any subject matter can now be researched to its fullest. I hear of companies struggling with problems that seem to be "new," and yet they find solutions in documents published five to 40 years ago.

Most of the technology that we use today is not new technology, but rather an innovative new application of existing technology. Electronic technology was developed in the early part of this century, but was never commercially utilized. Now it is being put to use on a commercial basis and the applications are being modified for patents. The technology for CD ROM systems is not new, but commercial use of the technology is. All the components of my computer system, stereo system and security system are less than two years old and yet they are considered obsolete technology. In reality, it's not the technology that has become obsolete, but the application of the technology.

Companies are creating brain pools comprising Ph.D.'s from various institutions and organizations. The use of management consultants is growing at an astounding rate. Interestingly, many members of the brain pools are individuals who are no longer valued by their own organizations and choose to work for a specified fee for another organization. Why is it that these individuals can do so well outside their own company and yet have difficulty within their own?

The speed and accuracy by which information can be gathered, analyzed and redistributed today is astonishing. Within minutes, people from any part of the world can communicate with one another using several different methods. This allows all of us to make better, more informed decisions in our daily lives. Yet few individuals really access the systems that are available. We will explore why the systems may not encourage or allow communication and information gathering to occur in a typical top down management structure.

Downsizing

In recent years organizations have been involved in a process called *downsizing.* The process sounds great to the financial community because it promises lower costs. Downsizing created work for consulting firms and has been packaged in as many different forms as there are consultants. The objective is logical. You need to examine your corporate structure periodically, and determine the proper size of each functional area in relation to corporate goals. As organizations attempted the process, most were amazed at the improved financial performance over the initial phases. It appeared to be the boost many companies needed.

But take a closer look. Would the organization have been oversized if management had been doing its job in the first place? Would there have been a need to hire consultants to observe the organization if management was paying attention? Unfortunately, downsizing became a crutch for managers who were unable to make tough decisions on their own.

How many people have heard the sermon, "I don't agree but the consultants have recommended......." It wasn't until after the dust and the exuberance began to settle that management realized what may have happened. Many good employees left, taking advantage of early retirement incentives, severance packages and other arrangements. If the good employees are leaving and the mediocre or low performers are staying, a powerful message has been sent. The organization lost touch with the people, the heart of what made it powerful.

Downsizing was the fad for weak management. The real irony is that management collected bonuses for improved financial performance and thousands of employees collected unemployment for following management's direction.

Reengineering

The process of *reengineering* an organization is probably one of the better methods of eliminating non-value-added work. Many books have been published outlining this process and hundreds of consulting firms have become highly profitable by reengineering organizations.

The task of reengineering is simple. But the process of reengineering is difficult and complex. The basic analysis of the work flow through the organization is easy to map out using flow diagrams and charting. Work processes that can be eliminated, consolidated or automated are then identified. For each of the areas that can be changed, a specific plan of action is developed and implemented.

Reengineering can be as broad or as narrow as the organization chooses. The process can focus on a single area, such as procurement, or encompass every activity from managing customer relations to production to logistics to information systems and accounting functions. The ultimate goal is to eradicate non-essential activities from the business so that the remaining activities are highly focused on the mission of the organization.

But consider the effects of reengineering on individuals. Have you ever listened to consulting experts discuss reengineering? As they review each job, it is quantified into an FTE (Full Time Equivalent). Some jobs are .75 FTE's and others are 1.25 FTE's. I was once told that I was performing 2.50 FTE's. The statistical and impersonal nature of this language is degrading. Of course, managers and consultants are enamored by the FTE concept because they no longer have to refer to employees as people.

The intentions may be good in these areas. Unfortunately, the signs of whether an organization is ready for the change are often ignored. When this happens, morale drops and management doesn't understand why the process isn't working. Training, education and timing are basic elements that must be considered before initiating the reengineering process. More often than not, there has been limited success with this process because the driving factor-the employees-were left out of the equation.

Self-Directed Work Teams / Quality Circles

The early 80's went wild with the introduction of *quality circles* into the workplace. This was going to be the answer to beating the Japanese at their own game. American companies were so convinced that the secret for success was in quality circles that millions and millions of dollars were spent on training and implementation. People were told to work in groups, and were taught statistical process control and statistical quality control. Colleges and universities graduated engineers with a specialty in the quality field. Yet in less than ten years, over 80% of the quality circle programs that were started failed. The process was not working.

Self-directed work teams were the logical outgrowth of quality circles. This is an excellent concept which, if designed and structured correctly, can create a environment in which high performance can flourish. But the concept is not new. A brief review of the Native American cultures reveals that many tribal communities functioned in a manner that closely resembles self-directed work teams. You can search back in history and find many civilizations structured in a similar manner. When the Mayflower landed, the Native American culture was already practicing democracy and teamwork. And yet the people referred to as the Fathers of our Country are credited with the introduction of democracy two hundred years later. Not to mention that the Japanese received recognition for developing the team concept four hundred years later. Is there something wrong with this picture?

For a simple example of an effective self-directed work team that is also self disciplined, look at any healthy family. In any given household there are numerous tasks to complete: laundry, cleaning, cooking, housework, yardwork, grocery shopping, repairs, chauffeuring the children, and more. Most of the time, every family member knows how to perform nearly every task. When someone is gone, all the work gets done. Does the family have to select what they do based on expertise and gender? No, everyone just helps where they are needed. Why doesn't this happen in the workplace?

Although we may believe that we have struck on a new path for high performance, the reality is that we have slightly modified a social system that existed for centuries, and repackaged it for a business setting. Just like technology, the application is new, but the basic system from which it is derived is not. If the human element is addressed properly, this system offers tremendous potential.

Certification Processes

Certification processes are being integrated into business systems throughout the world. There are many advantages and there are some concerns. The establishment of the Chemical Manufacturers Association (CMA) Responsible Care program is one example. The program establishes very specific criteria that the manufacturer of a chemical must follow. This womb-to-tomb concept is excellent. The practical applications may be questioned because the system is only as reliable as the people who administer the process.

Quality certifications such as the International Standards Organization ISO 9000 quality standards and ISO 14000 environmental standards are again excellent programs. They establish minimum acceptable criteria for a reliable process to develop and manufacture goods and services. ISO 14000 establishes minimum acceptable criteria for performance in the environmental and safety areas. The programs demand consistency and strict processes. However, they do not ensure profitability, job security, or even quality. Responsible repeatability is the end result.

Numerous other recognition programs have been developed. Each has its own specific targeted activity. And companies flock to the schools to learn what to do to become certified. With all these certification programs, the criteria for strong performance is identified and outlined for implementation. Yet, the statistics don't always show better or continuous performance. In some segments only continued deterioration is stopped. To understand why many of these programs are not successful, look at the company's motivation for certification. Is ISO 9000 certification important because repeatable process is important? Or is ISO 9000 a useful marketing tool for foreign market penetration?

To understand the intrinsic value of these programs we need to look further into the intentions of the organization. These certification processes are not magical, but in many instances give justification and legitimacy to personal gains and provide nothing to the employees.

Compensation Systems

Anytime I look at a business publication, there is an article on new pay systems or a new development on how to improve compensation systems to gain better performance from all levels of employees. Each of these systems demonstrates how the process will increase productivity, lower costs, pay for performance and tie salary budgets to actual organizational gains.

Gain sharing and profit sharing are probably the two best known forms of alternate compensation systems. Each can be designed to be the full payment system for salary increases, or as an augmentation to an existing salary system. Specific measurable goals are identified. These are goals that employees can impact directly and they're usually stretch goals achievable with some difficulty. With a gain sharing system, the gains (lowered costs or higher earnings) are generally distributed to the employees according to a predetermined formula where the employees and the company each receive a portion. Under profit sharing, the employees receive a percentage of the profits generated by the company. A predetermined formula is used to determine the payout, normally a percentage of an employee's salary. Both of these methods can be effective and I have seen both work successfully and unsuccessfully.

Some organizations have developed an innovation slush fund. This method sets aside a budgeted number of dollars that can be distributed to specific employees at any point in time for a task or idea contributed by an individual. The reward is direct, simple and immediate.

Managers consistently make the mistake of designing systems that would motivate themselves without realizing the program does not satisfy employees' needs. The demotivation this can bring into the organization can effectively shut down employee involvement. Recent times have seen the tightening of goals and the introduction of more restrictions on the payout of various plans initially targeted for employees. As the rewards diminish or become more difficult to achieve, the desire to be successful will give way to frustration, especially when profits are increasing.

Empowerment

Empowerment is probably the newest and most misunderstood concept in use today. I do not fully understand it. But it's a money making fad for consultants and it's a desirable phrase in annual reports.

Picture this: The operations manager states, "I want to empower these people. That's the way we're going to get things done around here." In the next breath, "Where are the production and shipping reports? I'll see if these guys have been playing games with me again!" Then, "Go find me a consultant who can teach people about empowerment. I want them here within two weeks, no more than a four hour training session and at a cost less than $10,000. Now go do it." Then, "Who said we could use that shipping firm again?"

Does this sound familiar? Empowerment may be a great concept. I've seen program outlines that define the system and it sounds like empowerment would have an excellent impact. It appears to be nothing more than trusting your employees with the responsibility to get the job done right. Ego, territorialism, listening skills and patterned behavior all stand in the way. Is the problem of implementation attributable to the employees, or to management's behavioral styles? Closer analysis might reveal that the obstacles are scattered throughout the organization in the form of attitudes rather than systemic problems. We will review various management styles and how they can influence the success and failure of programs and systems attempted within the organization.

Alternative Work Schedules

This is a slow but very important change that is taking place in some organizations. Alternative work schedules need not cause problems in the work environment. Remember, what gets measured gets done. The eight-to-five routine doesn't guarantee that work gets done, or that your processes are efficient. It only means that everyone is present at the same time.

The needs of the family are changing as more and more two income households develop. Despite efficiency and productivity gains, it is increasingly difficult to buy a home and raise a family. Various sources indicate that as many as 80% of today's households send both spouses into the workplace. That means that there is minimal family life. Children are in daycare or staying home for lonely hours at a time. Remember when you were a child? The first thing you wanted to do when you got home was talk about the day's events. Each time a child speaks, it's the heralding of his or her experiences. But in many of today's families, there is no one home to share it.

Organizations have been slow to respond to the true needs of a family. They stress the need for adults to meet their work schedules, and not the needs of the children. Most organizations have a direct interest in the adults and will demonstrate it through employee assistance programs, group benefit plans and family activities. These forms of assistance can be helpful but I believe that more emphasis should be placed on daily family life to prevent problems rather than provide assistance after problems arise.

In recent years we have seen the emergence of 12-hour shift schedules to allow employees more free time. Smaller organizations have adopted other programs such as working four 10-hour days per week Others are now allowing flex time where employees can set their own schedules within given parameters. Some electronics firms I am familiar with are encouraging people in certain jobs to set up home offices and only come to the office for progress meetings. One company that I know of is allowing any employee who travels more than 50,000 miles in a year to take his or her spouse on some of the trips, and will pay for the family to take one trip during the year. A large law firm has a policy of allowing any employee within the firm to take three consecutive months off every seven years to rest, relax and catch up on family relationships.

Each of these variations is an attempt to accommodate a growing demand that employers are placing on employees. The norm for many organizations is not to respond. With our trend toward downsizing, reengineering and high unemployment in middle and upper management, corporations expect individuals to work 50-60 hours per week and put family needs second. Children are involved in school activities but the parents aren't there to share their experience. Children miss opportunities for involvement with community and civic functions because there is no one available to provide transportation. Children are consistently left alone both in the mornings and late afternoons.

The impact of the work schedule on family life has numerous effects, none of which are positive for the family or for society. Organizations need to respond to the needs of families before we produce a second generation of abandoned children.

Information Systems

The field of information systems is one of the more rapidly changing areas in today's business environment. This is also an easier change to make. It doesn't involve modifying people's behavior to reprogram a computer. The changes have developed in two general areas: information access, and information format and usage.

Virtually anyone can access information on various topics, subject matter, products, and services through the use of a PC in their home. Computers are enhancing industries like telemarketing to improve efficiency. People can interact with one another via the information highway and select services ranging from travel, to shopping, to interactive pornographic material. There is nothing sacred any longer. Anyone who claims that he or she can't find information on a specific subject matter no matter how obscure just hasn't learned to use the modern tools.

Organizations have made extensive use of these systems. The offerings are so varied and so broad that more time is often spent selecting the appropriate services to investigate than is needed to actually collect the information. Organizations have learned to restructure their accounting and financial systems so that they know exactly, on-line, the performance figures for each department and the total organization. My experience has been that it is more difficult to find someone to *analyze* all of the information correctly than it is to collect the information.

One emerging discovery is that more than just financial information needs to be measured. Remember what gets measured gets done? Some companies are now beginning to utilize information systems to analyze non-financial data that can be just as critical to organizational success. Examples of measurements in this area include downtime on specific equipment, measures of customer satisfaction, analysis of work loads throughout the day and week for both peak and non-peak hours, employee satisfaction, and more. In many instances the activities of the people and the equipment measured give more insight into root cause analysis than the measure of the financial performance.

In fact, in most organizations financial performance is the end result of the non-financial factors that commonly go unmeasured.

Employees can provide you with more analysis and trend data on non- financial systems than any other source. The information can be on-line and interactive. This form of information gathering and sharing is responsive, powerful and accurate. Discussions of some of the newer methods are included in the following sections.

Management and employees both have the right intentions. There are few people who purposely show up for work with the intent of determining how they can cause a problem. Not all of the new systems that have been touted and sold to businesses are poor. The systems in fact can be very effective. The most frequent root cause of failure or limited success with these systems is not the program, it's that people have been left out of the equation.

Training and educating people is not enough. The work environment must be structured in a manner that allows change to occur. Change must be an interactive process where people don't just participate, but are the driving force. Employee leadership is essential to the formula that determines the success or failure of all management endeavors. Most often the biggest obstacles to business improvement are personal management behaviors, and clinging to past structures that feed ego, dominance and territorial needs of management. It's difficult for people to be expected to perform their best in an atmosphere of unpredictability, haunted by the real possibility of abandonment by the organization and those they trust.

The increased incident of heart attack, stroke, high blood pressure and depression are alarming, and they are affecting more younger age groups than ever before. People are asking for retirement at earlier ages. Consistent low morale, poor communication and unacceptable expectations afflict employees and managers alike. Divorce rates are up, societal problems are not improving and interpersonal relationships are changing. We have the largest legal system in the world and it is overloaded. And it is my belief that this is all a result of the fad programs that leave people, conscience and heart out of the equation.

I was recently handed an article which cited a survey performed by the American Management Association. The article was brief and to the point: one-third to one-half of all companies have attempted downsizing or reengineering. Of these, 80% reported that morale has collapsed. Two-thirds showed no improvements in productivity, 30% show increased overtime costs and 22% found they had eliminated the wrong people. And negative attitudes almost always adversely affected customer attitudes.

Through the remainder of this book I will discuss specific systems that can be improved geometrically by a simple change of focus. Unproductive behavior and attitudes are the first areas to be discussed and the first steps to be taken. The results can come quickly. And people who try these techniques will find more satisfaction with the direction of their personal lives and professional careers.

SECTION 2

Identification and Analysis of System Failures

The purpose of this section is to help identify and understand why many good systems don't work, or have only limited success. As we take a closer look, the reasons may surprise you.

Most new systems and processes that are widely discussed and adopted look good on paper and perform well in sanitary trial situations. But when these processes are actually assimilated into the daily work environment, the process improvements begin to fail. Many mangers still believe that the best way to achieve an end result is to plan from where they are today. And in many instances this may be the appropriate process to follow. But when you initiate dramatic changes in the dynamics and culture of an organization, it's much better to plan from the idealistic result backward to today. This enables you to see barriers to your plan that are entrenched in the organization. Yes, you can plan a trip from physical point A to point B rather easily on a two dimensional road map; but in planning this type of multi-dimensional journey, traditional maps are no longer useful. A compass and sextant are your instruments.

Barriers to evolution often appear in the form of sacred cows or unwritten rules in the organization. Deeper insight will reveal that these barriers are some of the most stubborn underlying reasons for the failure of a good process system. These barriers are created by individuals through territorialism, ego, fear and dominance all of which exist in the family, in business management and in union leadership. In order to be successful, a planning process cannot ignore the fact that these barriers are real and have been destructive. To achieve successful implementation of an idealistic process, you must determine how to address the illnesses caused by these behaviors so the wounds can heal.

The company's loss of respect for the individual, and the employees' loss of loyalty to the organization is evidence that American businesses, by and large, are no longer managing organizations with conscience; the compassion and heart that once existed needs to be sewn back into the work environment. Reciprocal dedication between the individual and the organization has been replaced by, "What have you done for me lately?"

The healing process can begin with one individual. Then it can be spread to another and another. Countries don't make decisions; people do. Companies don't make decisions; the decision begins with one individual and spreads. Decisions can be dynamic or diseased. It's that simple. Individuals have the power of choice-the choice to move forward or stand still.

When people are not included in the process of change they feel no ownership or participation in the new process. If people don't participate, cures can't take place. Companies define success in terms of money. Top managers define success in terms of material rewards. Real success is much more. It includes the values of society and respect for the environment. The business world has lost basic human ideals and as a result individuals, our society, and our environment are all paying a hefty price for an improved bottom line. It's time for change and the change needs to begin within each of us. As we become adults we expect the freedom to help make choices, yet we also fear the responsibility and self-discipline of adulthood. Unfortunately many of us mask our true feelings in destructive disguises.

The goal of this book is to illuminate a path to the creation of work environments that allow high individual performance, and foster a non-destructive thought process that benefits the individual, company, family and community.

The Underlying Forces

The first step in correcting any system failure is to logically analyze the root cause of the problem. In our hurry to find quick solutions, we often disregard valuable information and/or refuse to consider facts that don't mesh with our personal value systems and thought processes. We rush to those areas where we can't be personally blamed and search for any place to affix the reason for failure.

As mentioned earlier, many processes and systems have been developed and refined to a point that they really should succeed. And each organization that tries these various programs experiences varying degrees of success. Generally the public relations message about the success of these programs far exceeds actual results.

There are a number of common reasons why we don't achieve the levels of performance we desire. *Often these reasons lie within ourselves and the boundaries and barriers we've allowed to control our thought process and behavior.* We will first look at some of the basic barriers common to all of us. Then we'll examine the effect of value systems on process design. Next we will review the personality traits we must deal with, and finally we will discuss how to reestablish new programs to create a dynamic organization with content, highly productive individuals. You will see that the more an organization nurtures individuals, the more personal power everyone achieves.

First Underlying Force: Fear

The gurus of Total Quality Management talk about driving fear out of the organization. In discussions with other managers I have found that everyone hears the phrase, but doesn't quite know what it means. We tend to relate fear to external forces such as mugging, fire, hurricanes, etc. There is an internal force that controls our emotion of fear that we try daily to ignore and camouflage. *We cannot drive fear out of the organization; we must create an environment and support system for people to drive fear from themselves. Only then is fear driven out of the organization.* Each of the forms of fear that I've recognized within myself and others appear to be interrelated. Some of these fears include:

Fear of Failure People are reluctant to try something new and different in their lives for fear of failing. This is also true in the work environment. Failure equates to loss of status, loss of job, loss of others' confidence in you. You must first learn to recognize that there is no such thing as failing if you grow as an individual by making that choice. Each endeavor is a learning experience. Some experiences achieve a desired result, some do not. We learn in both instances and this learning process improves our reasoning ability. Where is the failure in learning? Fear of failure leads to fear of new experience and learning.

Fear of Losing Others' Confidence We are weak when our self-esteem is based on what others think of us, rather than how we view ourselves. Employees and managers let exciting opportunity pass every day for fear of losing others' confidence. It is manifested as the "good old boy" network.

We play politics. We procrastinate. We ask others' opinions to get the preview feedback before we decide what action to take. How often have you seen people play the wait-and-see game? Their self-generated fear causes this to happen. To act would be taking a risk. Taking a risk can mean doing the wrong thing. And if that happens we could lose others' confidence in us and be viewed as a failure. (See how this negative feedback builds on itself?) Only you can lose confidence in yourself. Other's opinions are fleeting evaluations.

Fear of Being Considered Stupid or Foolish "If I make a mistake I might look foolish." You're right, you might. Get used to it. But after a mistake, you can also move forward and identify how the experience brought new information to light that enables you to continue working on the problem. I have found that telling stories about my mistakes not only makes others laugh but offers additional benefits—

- Others will begin to discuss their mistakes and we all learn more in the process
- My mistakes are no longer viewed —by me or by others—in a negative manner, but rather as a brief search for learning

Fear can and does shut down our drive to gain new experience. It even stops us from enjoying simple pleasures in life. How many people do you know who refuse to sing in public? Yet the same individuals sing with the radio in their cars. How many people do you know who refuse to dance? Refuse to try a new sport? These activities don't even have a risk, relatively speaking. Rather than being open and taking a new plunge, we close our minds and miss many opportunities, only because we imagine how others might view us.

Fear of Becoming Isolated From Others We also fear that if we lose others' confidence, they might begin to avoid us. That could mean not being invited to their parties, or to a company outing, or to play golf. When this fear takes control, you constantly worry, "What will others think?" First, if someone avoids you because of one mistake, it was probably a superficial relationship to begin with. The more interesting fact is that we often punish ourselves and imagine far more persecution than the members of the group assign to us. We let fear take over. We beat up on ourselves, creating the illusion that others are leaving us. Normally the loss of social contact is generated by our own behavior after an event rather than by how others view us.

We fail to share certain life experiences for fear of how others might perceive us. By doing so, we're projecting an image of what we think the other person prefers, rather than being authentic to ourselves and others. Projections are a set of false images that we turn on and off. When they are off there's an opportunity to create something new. But when projections are active, our energy is focused on maintaining the self deception. By turning the projector off we tap an immense reservoir of energy which enables learning and growth.

Fear of Being Deprived Emotionally, we equate deprivation with pain and suffering. It applies only to the poor, the losers, and the foolish of the world. We imagine that if we allow ourselves to make a mistake this could all happen to us. It's ridiculous, but it's a powerful self inflicted force which can prevent any person from achieving full potential. First you must understand that whether or not you think you are deprived only exists in your mind. No one else can ever determine what you feel deprived of. You make that choice. If you stop listening to the mind clutter of what you have to lose and may not be able to gain, your life will begin to make more sense and you'll begin to experience more contentment.

Examples of Fear-Based Motivation

Company Rules Take a look at the written guidelines for your organization. Nearly every set are written in a negative manner. If employees do X, they'll be punished. The phrasing provides a negative response to everything the organization perceives as bad behavior. Organizations need to understand that rules don't motivate people to perform well, they only reinforce the fear of punishment we carry from childhood.

Management Behavior I've been in too many offices where the phrase, "Fire 'im!" is uttered about anyone who doesn't comply with management's unwritten rules. The managers speak without regard to who is present. This kind of talk creates a subconscious fear in the audience that the boss may be referring to them some day without their knowledge. The word gets out quietly. And soon employees are afraid to take risks or attempt new ideas for fear of breaking the rules.

Loss of Job Another example was the testimony of a highly competent benefits manager. His boss had the habit of asking people, "Do you know who you're dealing with?" anytime the other party disagreed with him. The benefits manager told me he was not proud of himself as he often nodded his head yes to this question and internally said no. But he knew if he spoke truthfully he would open himself to subtle punishments and low salary increases.

I once worked for an individual who had been a drill sergeant in the Marine Corps. His only method of motivation was to scream. My co-workers and I got so weary of the public humiliation and public threats that we eventually became mindless puppets.

Another type of undermining supervisor sent nasty grams. The supervisor refused to define the rules, and always spoke pleasantly to his subordinates in conversation. But if a subordinate sent the supervisor anything in writing, he could be assured that he'd receive a nasty gram the next day critically assessing his comments. The supervisor also left the messages open so that the memo and response could be read by everyone as it wandered through the company mail. The subordinate never knew where he stood and became paralyzed with fear of breaking an unknown rule. Motivation by fear of losing the job is prevalent and highly destructive.

The Lifecycle of Fear Children are often raised in an atmosphere of fear. The fear comes from threat of punishment and from loss of approval. There are literally hundreds of books and articles on this topic. Children are more aware of the effects of fear based behavior than adults are.

Once we reach adulthood, the fears are endless. Just listen to conversation. Adults have fears of heights, of flying, of making the wrong comment, of losing a job, of being alone, and many other situations. When you question people about the cause of their fears, they often provide an empty, long winded excuse. The explanation changes nothing and doesn't resolve the fear. People don't know why fear is present, but it controls portions of their lives. Adult life is dominated by fear based behavior that stops our growing and learning processes.

Organizations need to concentrate more effort on recognizing that fear is an internally generated emotion based on unfounded perceptions. Fear is strongest in those individuals with the lowest self-esteem and the lowest levels of security. Fear blocks an individual's and an organization's ability to change and grow. It blocks the family from experiencing the beauty of itself. When an individual is hired into an organization, the whole person should be allowed to enter the group. Dealing with the unseen portions of the individual is as important as dealing with the visible portions. The visible portions are the illusion and image you've hired; the invisible portion is the substance you've hired.

Second Underlying Factor: Uncontrolled Ego

Uncontrolled ego is a powerful, often destructive force that can effectively block progress within organizations, families, relationships and communities. Ego has nothing to do with fear. Ego is not reserved for any single socio-economic class. Ego is more common in individuals who desire leadership, materialistic toys and recognition (three common goals of business and union leaders) but it exists at all levels of society.

Ego is a game of *top dog.* It's a win/lose battle in that the person with the ego must always win, regardless of the costs to itself and others. It's a lose/lose proposition as the battles become a war. When ego takes over, life is not about right and wrong, or about ethical or immoral behavior it's about winning at all cost. After the ego wins, it then participates in rituals and mind games to maintain its (perceived) superior position. I've listed some examples of ego based communication, along with some insights about how it affects the performance of individuals and organizations. You will recognize many examples in your daily life (to the extent that your own ego will allow you). It is relatively easy to identify people with an ego that is destructive to themselves, their families and their communities.

Ego becomes a collector of names and places. In conversations with ego-driven people, you will hear where they've been, where they are going next, who they know and how they can help you. A friend of mine introduced me to his new acquaintance. This acquaintance first asked where I lived. I told him I was renting while we were building a house. Then he wanted to know the builder's name so he could find me a better builder. Then he asked where I was building. When I told him, he immediately explained that I was going to the wrong part of town. I should reconsider my choice, he said, and buy a lot in an area where I could meet the *right* people, those who could do me some good. In just a matter of minutes he had informed me that every life choice I was making was wrong. When the conversation ended, I concluded that I had made the right decision not to build in his neighborhood.

Ego is always asking"What can you do for me?" The next time you go to a party, watch the number of people who introduce themselves and then ask where you work and what your position is. Answer that you're a vice president and you have an immediate friend. Answer that you are a janitor and you will be standing alone. Ego is always on a feeding frenzy like a shark.

Ego blocks the ability to communicate and function fully. Every word that is heard is filtered through the ego. Ego only hears what it wants to hear and disregards the rest of the information. Have you ever had the experience of people repeating only portions of what you stated to them? Have you ever watched as individuals repeat only the facts relevant to their point and disregard all other information? Have you ever watched people interpret facts in a manner that best serves their personal agendas? This type of communication does not solve problems but serves only to maintain an ego's self-deception. Rarely are decisions made, relationships improved, or action plans developed at the completion of the discussion. Any plans that result serve only the dominant ego in the group.

Ego is always showing its superiority. Once I was riding up a ski lift with two corporate executives. One looked down and saw two hikers on a trail beneath us. He immediately opened the window and spit on the hikers. This was a publicly respected, intelligent individual in his late forties, spitting on people he didn't know just because he could.

Have you observed that there are certain individuals who must be first and last to speak in a meeting? Have you ever met with someone who first redefines the purpose of your meeting and then feels compelled to conclude it in a manner that fits his or her personal agenda? Meetings with people like this can only conclude when their ego is satisfied. Once again results, action plans and relationships are unimportant unless they serve the dominant ego.

Ego wears a shroud of delusion and self-deception. This clouds all interactions and experiences of the ego-dominated individual. Ego will reject anything that begins to tear down its mask and reveal the true self. Criticism is met with anger or simply ignored. The ego's mind filters all that is seen and heard on a constant mission of damage control. This effort wastes tremendous energy that could be put to productive, rather than protective, use. Ego will not accept the truth or most of what is authentic about you. Ego prefers not to be alone, for fear of an unflattering self search. These realizations will be in conflict with ego.

Ego communicates through, "Speak, for I am listening (to myself)." When talking with a person with a big ego, you often become a listener just by taking a breath during a sentence. And you will remain the listener until ego decides that the conversation is completed. Remember, ego must always have the last word. What you have to offer is only important to the extent that the ego can benefit from the information.

Ego can't listen because it hurts. Ego screens information through an invisible filter created in the mind, and it's very effective. Much of the dominant behavior we experience stems from these filters. Listening to the whole story reveals more than the ego can handle. The listening process is finely developed with a broad range and many layers of filters to reject the information that doesn't satisfy the ego. Have you ever repeated a point to an individual over and over again, only to have him claim he's never heard it before?

Ego will always prove superiority. In ego's relationships with children, with employees and with clients, the conversation always comes back to ensuring that everyone knows ego is just a little bit better. Ego will always resort to politics, terminations, violence or other means to cnsure everyone understands its superiority. If you ask ego probing questions that require direct and concise answers, you will eventually be verbally attacked on a personal level so that ego can reestablish its superiority.

I recently hired an attorney to handle a personal matter (by the way, I would not recommend this to anyone). During one conversation I repeatedly asked him about his strategy for our case. I never could see the path he was trying to follow. Shortly into the conversation he verbally attacked me stating that I lived my life by pushing others around so that I could always get my way. He was trying to reestablish his superiority by attacking me.

I never received an answer or an explanation of his strategy, just a demonstration of his superiority. After the legal process was completed, he actually sent me copies of letters he had received from some of the defendents attorneys congratulating him on doing an excellent job. His ego was satisfied by his peers. I thought he was mediocre. His opinion of himself was very important and could only deal with information that agreed. Shortly after the close of the ordeal, his wife left him. Apparently, the superiority syndrome was not limited to the office.

Ego is always immersed in appearances. Ego will always have the right labels on clothing. Ego chooses friends based on their social status. Ego always has the latest toys and will invite you over to see them. Egos always look for greener grass in toys, clothing, housing, friends or sex. Ego doesn't care about the consequences of short-sighted decisions because ego can only function in the here and now of others' perceptions. The toys wear out. The clothes wear out. People lose their jobs or move. There is always a better neighborhood. Choosing a sex partner based on physical appearance rather than emotional compatibility must become a challenge as people physically begin to age. Thus, the birth of plastic surgery!

I love watching two or more egos in a meeting. It's so boring if there is only one. When one ego is present there is no conversation, just a monologue. But two or more egos create exciting entertainment. Each ego feels compelled to play the one-up game. The first ego speaks. As he/she takes a breath, the second ego becomes the speaker and adds to the first ego's comments. When ego number two takes a breath either the first ego will regain the floor, or if he's slow a third ego will jump in and add another thought to the first two. Meetings that should take 15 minutes or less take two hours or more. Generally no decisions are made and no specific focus is defined. There is only a collection of thoughts surrounding tough issues that they are all afraid to attack. Then fear-based activity comes into play. If you want to have real fun, put a grease board in the room with one less pen than there are egos present. Tension ensues because two egos cannot be clearly identified due to a shared color. How can an ego take the coveted credit when it's forced to share?

One individual that is wonderful at demonstrating ego reminds people that if they follow the rules and do a good job, they will be promoted like him. He constantly changes the rules of the game without notice. Why? First he establishes the rules to show his superiority. After announcing the rules to those who were not promoted, he quietly checks with his boss as to what the rules should be. In the conversation he will discuss his own ideas. When the conversation is completed, he notifies everyone else of the new rules. But the notification does not take place in a group setting. He contacts each person individually, involves them in a discussion where they both conclude that a rule change is needed. In this manner, he makes each person think they are actually a part of the decision process.

At one time a co-worker of mine was trying desperately to set up a new department within our company. All the plans were written out and after receiving approval from the Promoted One, he proceeded. During the next twelve weeks the guidelines were changed a total of *six times!* By week sixteen he was criticized for not making enough progress and another individual was hired from outside the organization to develop this department "correctly." Then the Promoted One openly discussed his disbelief of my co-worker's unacceptable performance in setting up the new department.

These are all representations of the ego-based behavior. By referring to himself as the Promoted One, he was measuring his self worth as superior to all others. He frequently mentioned his material possessions to establish that he had the right external materialistic symbols of success. By criticizing others' work he again establishes his superiority. By consulting with the boss for approval on every detail, he demonstrates that he can't stand alone—for without praise and admiration the ego starves. Replacing my co-worker on this project met his need to reestablish superiority.

Although this individual actually had some good intentions, his ego became well known within the organization. Behind a closed office door he delighted in others' failures. During conversations he omitted facts that didn't support his point and distorted information to better his position. If facts got in his way, he just ignored them. And whenever a crisis situation arose, he stepped forward to save the day.

One of the lessons I learned from the Promoted One was that in his zeal to "do good," he couldn't stand silence. Try this with a strong ego. Answer questions with less than three words and then wait. The ego you are speaking to will fill in all the details because he/she cannot stand silence. The Promoted One also taught me a second lesson; tell the truth and anything you say can be used against you.

Ego-based behavior is obvious to everyone. And egos also recognize it in others. This behavior creates many of the sacred cows and unwritten rules which undermine the organization. These obstacles prevent both optimum decisions and optimum performance. At home, socially and at work, ego blocks the process flow. Systems, relationships and people can't grow when they are forced to deal with ego satisfaction.

Third Underlying Factor: Territorialism and Dominance

Territories can be clearly spotted within an organization. They define the organization's structure, determine who is in power, and define the unwritten rules. Territories lead you to dominant individuals and can delineate process and task.

I believe that people become territorial and dominating due to their feeling of inadequacy. To overcome this inadequacy, individuals must establish territory and dominance under their own rules. It is a self-made barrier developed by the individual for protection. The barriers create rippling discord throughout the lives of others, both at work and at home.

Being dominant means constantly proving yourself to yourself, through the destruction of others. Observe nature. Animals are constantly fighting for dominance. Playing the dominant role means you must create conflict. Without conflict, dominance cannot be established. Don't confuse constructive discussion involving conflict with this type of destructive conflict.

Dominant individuals in group settings purposefully create disruption. They will not allow credit to be taken by others in the group without giving approval. Doing so does not fit their self-perception. Dominant behavior reinforces itself through judging others and always coming to the conclusion that others do not measure up to the standards created in a dominant's mind.

Have you ever given a presentation or presented a project only to have an individual criticize peripheral components such as layout, format, spelling and grammar yet never offer an opinion on the subject matter, recommendations or conclusions? Meet Mr./Ms. Dominant. If the substance is good they will divert focus to other items quickly to point out errors.

Dominant types protect their territories. When managers are moved within the organization, they will often leave behind a treasure chest full of errors and incomplete work. A dominant personality cannot address these issues in a public manner so issues and errors are hidden in hope of non-discovery. And the system works pretty well—until this person is forced to abandon their territory.

I had the experience of working with one person who epitomizes a dominant, territorial individual. He was the only individual that would wait until a meeting to point out errors in information that had been distributed prior to the meeting. He was respected for his intellect and equally despised for his rude and undermining behavior. As this manager was moved within the organization, each group he left behind went from being one of the best groups in the industry to one of the laziest, inept groups in the industry—*in his opinion.* His opinions would change rapidly and grow more vocal as the treasure chest was uncovered. He then pointed out each individual's faults, never accepting any personal responsibility.

Dominants don't want you to know the rules. They make the rules up as the need arises. But there is one consistent behavior—the public correction of others' mistakes. The more public the correction can be, the more it pleases the dominant personality. Dominants create the feudal system that exists in industry. They are the rulers. Those who don't cross them are rewarded with protection within the territory. Those who do not obey will be exiled and publicly humiliated whenever possible.

To protect territory and to maintain dominance, these individuals fuel office politics. But they are not generally recognized as the manipulators. Dominants go from office to office, looking for an audience and quietly pass on partial truths to get the organization unsettled. Then they back out of the picture and wait until the right time to help save the day and reestablish their dominance.

Teamwork, motivation and communication are very difficult to develop in an atmosphere that includes dominance. Creativity will die. Have you ever been in an organization where there is a momentum building to introduce a new process or product? People get excited and contributors are recognized for excellent ideas. Then Mr./Ms. Dominant shows up. What happens? The room becomes quieter, and criticism of the new process or product begins to develop. Within an hour the whole project needs to be attempted again, the right way, with Mr./Ms. Dominant taking the lead to prevent these silly errors from happening again. Sound familiar? When unwritten rules about *who is included* in new process or product design are violated, the project is doomed from the start.

With this behavior erupting in an organization, no wonder good systems don't have a chance. Communication can't take place directly between individuals within the organization. It must clear Mr. Dominant before entering the territory. Freedom of speech is nearly taken away from those who work for this individual.

How do you think this individual functions as a parent or spouse? The same behavior is present, but may manifest itself as violence, jealousy, and emotionally abusive behavior.

The Effects of Undermining Behaviors

Lack of Direction Excellent management tools are available to us. So there's no excuse for an organization not to have defined a focus for its future, and for employees to be unaware of their individual roles in achieving success. Yet most organizations still lack direction and focus. Change is a very slow process. If the components of a management system are correct then failure is likely due to fear, ego, territorialism, dominant behavior, and other personal interests. These unseen barriers will prevent individuals and organizations from achieving their full potential. These negative forces create a flurry of activity, creating a rush to nowhere.

Lack of Focus Remember that *what gets measured gets done.* Well-intentioned people can create unbelievable chaos without recognizing what they've done. Within today's organizations, management thinks up new projects on a daily basis. And the projects are usually valid. However, everything is easily accomplished by those who don't have to perform the work. There is a lack of priorities in today's organizations. There's often no measurement of resource utilization. Priorities change after each management meeting, and when a new best seller is released. Work becomes less accurate and less meaningful because people don't know the priorities—the very objectives they are supposed to focus on and complete.

Within one organization I asked many people what they considered to be their current priorities. The engineering group had to ask the engineering manager for the answers because they didn't know. It would appear relatively simple for a small group of engineers (ten employees total) to focus on key results. With a budget of 17 million dollars, you'd think the company would be very clear on how those dollars were to be spent. When I asked the engineering manager how he determines his department's priorities his response was, "Whichever VP walks into my office first in the morning." This group had talented people. Each one could have been an excellent leader. They had excellent systems to accomplish their goals. The effects of fear, ego, dominance and territorialism can circumvent even a strong foundation, and create and maintain a chaotic environment for both employees and the company.

Lack of Balance in Personal and Professional Life

Organizations are demanding more and more from people. The work week is extending to 50-60 hours as a norm rather than an exception. Couples are working extended hours, leaving children at home alone. Their defense is that "the children will be fine." Yes, the children probably will be fine physically. But who is looking out for their emotional well-being? Single parents are coping with an unbelievable burden today. In the business world, we are becoming so focused on career paths and earning money that the very basics of life are being ignored. Some companies allow employees to freely shuffle their hours to meet family demands. This is called trust. Many organizations, however, require that employees schedule vacation or sick time if they need to take a child to the doctor or go to see a school play. This is called cruelty and greed. I have taken the time to attend as many of my children's activities as possible, often with disapproval of my peers.

We no longer have the time to enjoy simple pleasures. Adults don't have any excess time; professional careers are consuming it all. When time does become available, it's spent socializing with the "right people" or entertaining to show off our latest toys.

We need to balance the needs of the workplace and home life again, and it's not that difficult to accomplish. But we must first learn to recognize the enemy, where it lies and how to address it. You will find time and again that the enemy is within—fear, ego, dominance and territorialism..

Lack of Employee Loyalty and Commitment The collapse of employee loyalty and trust in today's organizations is no surprise. Past performance no longer counts. "What have you done for me today?" is the only thing that matters to the new management style. How can organizations and individuals perform, or even survive in this type of environment? Where there is a lack of commitment and trust between entities, it's almost impossible to develop high performance levels for yourself or others.

The Effects On the Individual

When an individual becomes unbalanced in life, a search process is often activated. We search for more happiness, but equate that happiness to a new house, a new car, a new job or even a new spouse. Unfortunately when we acquire the new item, we are still carrying the same emotional baggage and destructive thought processes that drove us to the search. We don't spend quality time on ourselves. We don't spend quality time with our spouse or children. Our work performance demands more time, but often with poorer results. To begin a path toward a content, high-performance lifestyle we must first understand ourselves and the effects that fear, ego, dominance and territorialism have on our lives. We must each recognize these negative forces and learn how to deal with them effectively before we can make progress.

In the coming sections, you'll learn how to build both the new individual performance environment and the new organization.

SECTION THREE

Changing Paradigms

Building the Balance

MANAGEMENT	EMPLOYEES
Commitment	Productivity
Guiding	Communication
Listening	Intelligence
Taking No Credit	Zero Defects
Accepting Accountability	Self-Directed
No Territory	Supportive
Honesty	Multi-Functional
Supportive	Excellence
Induce No Fear	Informative
Focus on Non-Financial	Financial Results
Common Good	Responsive
Balanced Life	Balanced Life

Is Change Really Necessary?

Absolutely. A major shift is taking place throughout society, but few have recognized the need to address the implications of this shift. We are in the midst of a quiet revolution. There's a growing emphasis on *balance* in life and work. This quiet revolution will usher in a more positive society, with stable families and wise business guides. Employee leadership and management guides will emerge to shape powerful organizations that operate with a conscience and a heart.

Change is here to stay, and no one will escape it. Each time you read about a new product, it has already begun its progression to obsolescence. It may be one year or twenty years but its death is inevitable.

Throughout society you can see signs of change and you can see signs of disease. The use of drugs and alcohol is epidemic within our society. Adults tend to view the problem as one of teenage rebellion. But where did the teenagers learn this behavior? Children are no more than a reflection of their environment. Many children live with part-time parents, or parents who don't accept responsibility for their actions, or parents who cope with stress through drug and alcohol abuse, or parents who can only teach materialism and not the values of life, or parents who live their lives wearing multiple masks. With these role models, what kind of behavior can we expect from our children?

We have become a society of greed and consumption. Success is now measured by the size of your house, the brand names you buy, your job title(s) and the number of expensive toys you own. This type of success is a fleeting, outward sign of borrowing and consumption that doesn't truly measure how successful a person's life may be. Perhaps you've witnessed what happens to people who lose their material possessions. Many of these individuals are simply victims of circumstances such as plant closings, layoffs, reorganizations, reengineering, downsizing and other new tools of business. These people often tragically discover that their entire self-image has been based on their professional identity, and they don't have a clue about who they really are. When the external symbols disappear, it's time to face the inner self—and many times they can't find it. The too common result is divorce, depression, criminal behavior, bitterness and many other uncharacteristic behaviors. This is the outward expression of a wretched screaming spirit.

Organizations generally do not take an active role in developing an environment conducive to the long term betterment of the company, the employees, the community and society. The tools are available, but quite often the implementation is superficial. For effective change, everyone must participate. Change directed at middle and lower level employees will result in minimal success, if any at all.

I observed one organization that epitomized this behavior. The company published statements about "serving the best interests of the community." These messages brought positive public attention and stimulated large monetary donations to all the major civic activities in the community. Ads appeared on television depicting employees of this organization as your common neighbors. But at the same time the company did not have an emergency response plan and was storing thousands of gallons of carcinogenic, corrosive and/or flammable chemicals on a site positioned within a residential and retail area of the community.

Another organization published a list of all of the benefits available to its employees. But management quietly complained about the high cost of these benefits behind closed doors. Over time, benefits slowly disappeared from employees as management increased benefits and stock plans for its top executives. The costs of the top management benefits were actually greater than those of the programs being taken from employees under the pretense of "cost reductions" or "competitive requirements."

One company had a very serious and obvious problem that employees could see. Of eight top managers, one had a heart attack and three others were on high blood pressure medication. Five were actively seeking other employment. Three were trying desperately to negotiate a severance package to leave the company. Corporate management viewed this group of divisional managers as weak and unable to take the organization to the next level. None of the divisional managers were offered assistance. None of the managers were given honest feedback. But they did receive verbal lashings, avoidance, and eventual replacement. The new management immediately initiated action programs that had been developed—but not yet implemented—by the original division managers. Ultimately, corporate management credited "new blood" with the rescue and cited them as examples that all others should learn from.

I distinctly remember a situation within one organization that I thought was the ultimate blow. An employee's wife had outpatient surgery on an emergency basis. The supervisor gave the employee a warning for being late to call in his absence. The next day the employee took a day off to stay home with his wife and two preschool aged children. When he returned to work his supervisor suspended him for absenteeism. For the next several years people asked why this man was so bitter toward the company.

Dissatisfaction and deception have become a way of life. Within the middle-aged group of employees everyone wants to retire as early as possible. They want of out today's business world. Yet older employees seem content and at times remorseful of having to retire. The most balanced view, and the one that I happen to agree with is, "I want to work for the rest of my life until I decide to quit, hopefully in my eighties. But between now and then I want the quiet time to know myself, experience nature and the beauty of life, the time to know and enjoy my children, and the time to love and serve my best friend and spouse. I want to share my abilities with others in the community and learn something from everyone I meet." Why should all this true enjoyment have to wait until my life is nearly over?

Spirituality is experiencing a resurgence within society at an accelerated pace. People are learning meditation. People are seeking alternatives to modern medicine. The methods and knowledge of ancient native cultures are suddenly resurfacing. And for those who have sought these alternatives there is a renewed sense of self-esteem and contentment they have never experienced before. The so-called *new age* image is crossing socio-economic lines. There is nothing new about this. It is happening because people are discovering practices that are hundreds of years old and finding that they are valid. Outlets offering spiritually centered merchandise are appearing on the main streets in middle America. Consortiums are developing to teach the ancient native methods. And the methods are working. Somewhere over time we lost touch with some of the most magical basic fundamentals of life.

To begin the restructuring we must—if only for a moment—*clear our minds.* Clarity is absolutely necessary in order to let new information flow into our minds without being tainted by our old filters. For the restructuring to take place, our focus must be placed on four key areas and in this order: self, business methods and tools, community, and sustainable resourcefulness.

STEP ONE:

Who am I?

Changing the Paradigm of a Typical Manager

I remember awakening on a brisk morning just after sunrise. The beauty of the Sedona landscape was coming alive, as if the sun was finger painting in a deliberate manner. Every few minutes the colors would change, the setting would appear different and yet I had not moved. Momentarily, the past had vanished from my mind and I could see with a clarity that I had not experienced before.

Soon my wife was moving about the room and a friend who had come to visit was making coffee. The piano was playing and there was laughter filling the room. I realized that I was the one laughing and my wife and I were playing *Heart and Soul.* We hadn't done this for years. I suddenly realized that my alcohol intake had been eliminated for a week and my cigarette habit had dropped to nearly zero.

Within an hour the three of us were traveling to a hiking area to experience the countryside and view some of the many beautiful Native American ruins around the area. The experience was passing like a dream. We walked nearly five miles into a canyon area. Yet it seemed like a very short stroll. I could feel my senses coming alive. The colors were vivid, the scents were clear and distinct, the plant and animal life seemed to speak to me.

As we neared the end our short trek, we climbed up a hillside and explored the beauty of an ancient cliff dwelling. As we stopped and sat down, all time vanished. My senses were so alive I was trembling. As the warm sun beat down on the red rock I could only gaze across the landscape. An hour passed, but I felt I had experienced a minute at the most. As we left the area and began our drive back into town I remember feeling as if I was leaving home.

This experience never left me. I began to ask myself, "Who am I?" And surprisingly, the answers began to come very quickly (and they are still coming today as I write this—). For the first time in my life I felt I was meeting me. Each thought I had about who I actually was solidified by my previous thoughts. And as each thought solidified, an old perception began to disappear. As each new revelation became clearer and broader, something interesting happened. The person I met did not have a title, social status, street address or investment portfolio. This person had a very clear identity—a sense of values and beliefs—very different from the physical and social identity that I would be returning to at the conclusion of our stay.

One of the more important discoveries I made was that I was my own worst enemy. Daily I fed the enemy through political games, dominating others, validating my self-worth by devaluing others, and filling my mind with talk about how to win in a situation or manipulate an individual. My ego was strong and had completely clouded my view of those around me at work, and at home. It had blocked my understanding of what was important in my life. I can only imagine how many lives I had touched in a negative way.

To begin a process of change anywhere—at home, in the work place, in the community, or in government—you must begin within your inner self. That's the one and only change over which you have complete control. Many phases are required in order to make this change. It's not easy, because for years your life has been structured around untruths about yourself. These feed on one another and cause the development of behavior which exists only to strengthen more untruths. Before you know it, you are not you, you are acting out your untruths and following the behavior that keeps them alive.

Controlling Your Ego

You live what you create. High blood pressure, strokes, ulcers, depression, anxiety, divorce, troubled children, and betrayal are all conditions that you bring on yourself. We all have an image of who we think we are and rarely is it accurate. We choose to unleash our egos and they proceed, slowly but surely, to destroy us. We've contracted an infectious disease, and its primary symptom is *wanting*— wanting that focuses only on physical possessions. We let our egos tell us who we are and then we feed the disease to gain that particular status. The disease shuts down our ability to think, to interact and to relate to the world around us. Everything we see and do is clouded. Only those experiences that satisfy the ego are allowed to penetrate the veil. We become entombed in a casket of comfort, but find that we can never rest because we're carrying it on our backs. And the energy diverted to this burden cannot be used for any meaningful activity.

You must learn to recognize the ego within yourself and the signs of destruction that it creates in you and those around you. Ego works in a manner that requires you to prove others wrong in order for you to be right.

Here are some examples of what I am talking about. Have you noticed how many people constantly dole out excuses and feel the need to explain things? Excuses and explanations are the same thing. We use them to justify what our wanting ego needs. There is always an excuse to explain why you couldn't attend your child's school program. And there are other excuses why you couldn't hit the production targets your supervisor asked for, why your department didn't perform according to expectations, and why the company didn't meet its objectives. There are also excuses to justify why you can't stop drinking and why this just isn't a good time to stop smoking. Other explanations justify why you purchased the new BMW over the used Cutlass. And of course it's easy to explain why you needed a bigger house. You can explain everything, use all the excuses you can think of, but it doesn't change the facts.

Everyone can think of people who use these excuses regularly. Just listen to yourself at work or at social occasions and count the number of times you exhibit the same behavior. Write down every excuse you use for one week and see how many pages you fill; then look at how empty and hollow these excuses really are.

Stop making excuses and accept the fact that you are responsible for everything you do, regardless of the outcome. Recognize that your ego must be controlled or your potential and the potential of those around you will remain untapped. As you keep track of your excuses you will begin to recognize the pattern and stop using them.

There are some interesting acronyms for EGO:

Easing **G**od **O**ut
Erasing **G**oodness **O**penly
Executive **G**reed and **O**mnipotence

You can probably think of some other good ones.

Controlling Fear (**F**eeling **E**xcuses **A**re **R**eal)

Meet Mr. or Ms. Can't. Our gender determines which one we are. Our unfounded fears have powerful control over our thoughts and actions. Listen to yourself and the people around you, and track the number of fears you encounter. But listen closely, because one of the strongest is the fear of what others will think of us. Fear generally appears with an excuse:

"I can't dance," *because I'm afraid people will think I look foolish.*
"I'm afraid of the dark," *because I think things will appear that can't be seen in the light.*
"I'm afraid of losing my job," *because it is my identity (If this is the case you have a lot of work to do).*
"I'm afraid of flying," *because I am not in control.*
"I'm afraid of speaking in front of people," *because I might not get their approval.*
"I'm afraid to tell my boss what I think," *because he might retaliate.*

As you come to retrain your thought processes, you will understand that no one can take anything from the authentic you unless you allow it.

Overcome these fears. The energy and power you have diverted to them can be converted to positive energy to make your life come alive. Who cares what others might think? Any negative feedback is generally just a response from another fearful person who is actually envious. The next time your spouse asks you to dance, do it. The next time you want to talk to your boss, do it. Look for an opportunity to share an experience with a small group of people and then do it.

The next time you see a sign for a clothing-optional beach, do it. You will be absolutely amazed at how quickly fears can subside, and make way for new experiences in your life. *You must confront your fears and write down a simple affirmation you will take to rid them from your life forever.*

Controlling Dominance

Dominance takes on many forms in our lives. At times it may be appropriate to use dominant forms of behavior, but it's rarely effective. Dominance never offers solutions; in fact, it inhibits solutions. It's a common behavior that we use to exercise control at the expense of others' self-esteem. Dominance drains people of energy and replaces it with fear. Dominance and ego are different characteristics, but manifest themselves in a similar manner, with the same destructive effect on ourselves and others.

Why is it so easy for some people to dominate others? It's because they recognize that most people have deeply rooted fear of consequences. Dominant behavior is quite prevalent and powerful in the organizations that have implemented downsizing. With fewer people, longer hours and higher pressure, each individual's energy level and strength is decreased. Beaten back, they look around at all those who have been terminated, and the thousands of qualified workers who would give anything for their job. How do they begin to feel? Trapped.

And the dominant individuals know this. I have actually heard managers discussing that the best way to gain maximum performance is to fire two or three workers and hope that it takes them more than a year to find another job, and preferably at a lower wage. Those remaining will work harder in fear of finding themselves in the same situation. In effect, fear in others is the friend of the dominant individual.

Dominant individuals develop loyalty by generating fear. They have power and they take advantage of opportunities to publicly humiliate others. Dominants are the ones who take information distributed prior to meetings, find something that they can point out as a fault, and then wait until the meeting to raise the issue. They don't discuss it privately with the presenter because that would destroy their opportunity to humiliate and reestablish their dominance in a public forum.

Think for a moment how children are treated in so many situations. Their lives can be a very frightful experience. They are governed by negative rules in nearly every setting. Schools, teachers, parents, coaches, and babysitters each have rules; all of them designed to deliver a prescribed punishment if disobeyed. None of these rule makers talk to one another, so the child can be exposed to varying sets of rules every day which might contradict one another from setting to setting. *As you observe dominant behavior, confront it immediately regardless of the setting. Once a dominant individual realizes that his or her game is exposed, the game is no longer effective.*

Controlling Territorialism

Individuals who are dominating are usually also territorial. They constantly seek to establish their territory within the whole, and then reinforce it using every conceivable means. Watch these individuals during a restructuring process. They cannot cope with the change. They will continually work behind the scenes to gain support for their opinion that the organization is now disorganized.

In social situations, we also define our own personal territory. When people stand too close, handle our possessions, or reach out to hug or touch us in a friendly manner we get uncomfortable.

We are not a sharing society. Territorialism begins when we as children witness our parents' actions. We continue the practice well into our adult lives. We expend great energy defending our territory—energy that can be better used in other activities.

When you see territorial behavior, confront it. Call it what it is, and refuse to abide by its rules. As the controlled groups and excluded groups begin to rebel—constructively—the territorial behavior will begin to fade and eventually disappear.

We cannot begin to use new systems and tools effectively with employees in the business setting until we first recognize and correct the destructive behaviors that current leadership perpetuates in the work environment. And we cannot begin to improve relationships with the important people in our lives until we recognize and begin to correct the destructive patterns we've learned. The ego must be put to rest if we intend to stop having self-recriminating talks with ourselves every day.

It's also important to learn not to fear failure. Try to view it only as a learning experience that improves our knowledge and judgement.

As we begin to recognize these patterns and their fallout in our lives several interesting changes will begin to occur. You will find that people can no longer intimidate you or take away your drive and energy. You will find that people can no longer manipulate you into doing things you don't want to do. Your children will become less problematic and begin to grow and learn at a rate you didn't think possible. The new you will recognize and release destructive behaviors and begin to grow. You will be sought out as a leader and guide for all types of activities, for the new you will exude a self confidence and contentment that is inspiring to others. You will find that people will begin to recognize the wisdom you've gathered—a mix of strength, compassion, honesty and caring behavior that is powerful and influential without taking or dominating. Your satisfaction and contentment will build on itself, and those around you will grow and learn from your strength.

STEP TWO:

Who am I interacting with?

Recognizing Value Systems

Managers and supervisors often fail to recognize the basic driving forces within the people they deal with every day. Each person's individual value system, when tapped correctly, will open the individual to positive change, creativity and self-directed attitudes. Unfortunately, failure to recognize these value systems often leads to confusion, mistrust and low levels of performance. Individual value systems can be recognized with just a little effort on the manager's part. What is a value system? It's the basic foundation that a person uses to determine what is and is not proper within every interaction in their lives. Since people exist at different levels of psychological development, it's important to understand how these values shape their attitudes toward work, policies and programs and life in general.

Dr. Charles Hughes of *The Center for Value Research* in Dallas, Texas, has dedicated his professional career to the study of value systems and how they impact individuals in the workplace. In one of his earlier books *Making Unions Unnecessary,* Dr. Hughes offers a practical guide to understanding value systems. The following segment on value systems is an overview of Dr. Hughes' philosophy which has been previously published. More information on value systems can be obtained directly from Dr. Hughes at:

The Center for Value Research
8848 Greenville Ave.
Dallas, TX 75243

"This section borrows significantly from the writings of Dr. Charles L. Hughes of the Center for Values Research, Dallas, Texas and his applications of the theories of Dr. Claire W. Graves."

Value System 1 - Reactive The human being is born without a value system and believes nothing about any aspect of life. In addition to infants, adults with brain deterioration, brain damage and those in poverty hold no value systems. People in Value System 1 react to warmth, pain, hunger, but not to other individuals as human beings. Therefore, they will not be found in the work world.

Value System 2 - Tribalistic Beyond the reactive state people develop into a state of tribalism in which the values held by the tribe come from a chieftain who may be the boss, parent or spouse. The content of their work is not important, but the leadership from the boss or chieftain is. People who exist at the tribalistic level of psychological development prefer strong leadership: a boss who tells them what to do and provides recognition when the work is done properly. Money and the other things necessary in life are for the purposes of existing. The formal educational level of the tribalistic individual is quite likely to be low. Studies show that many low income employees are primarily tribalistic and few, if any, professionals or others with advanced education and reasonable affluence are significantly tribalistic.

Tribalistic employees respond best to simplistic graphic and personalized communication. They tend to read little but respond to pictures and appreciate eye-to-eye communication. As a result, many handbooks are completely inappropriate for communication with a tribalistic workforce.

Tribalistic employees prefer routine tasks and find a great deal of satisfaction in repetitive activities which have a rhythmic routine. It is fortunate that 25% of the employee population is primarily tribalistic because industry offers so many tribalistic jobs. It would be a disservice to place a tribalistic person into a job offering task variety or job enlargement. A tribalistic employee should be placed with a good chieftain and other employees who hold the same values.

Performance appraisal systems often overlook the tribalistic values. Performance must be linked to the tasks and values given to the tribe. The process must be group-centered and determined by the chieftain. In this value system, the performance of the group and the relationship to the boss are appraised more than the individual.

Pay and benefits for these employees should be based on automatic increases determined by the immediate supervisor and related to length of service and membership in the tribe. Merit and incentive pay are perceived as irrelevant. This group focuses on receiving benefits at the time they are needed.

Motivation centers around recognition from the boss for doing a good job, not from the job itself. Continuous stroking is needed, not job enrichment. These people want to get along, not ahead.

While these systems may be uncomfortable for the personnel manager and management in general, it is right for this group of employees.

Value System 3 - Egocentric This is the group of rugged individualists who are tough, aggressive and a frequent source of problems. These people are suspicious and tend to engage in disruptive behavior. They need jobs that don't tie them down, and a supervisor who can manage this behavior. This person places himself ahead of all others and generally has difficulty in dealing with the constraints of society and rules.

Communications must be direct, authoritarian and explain the consequences of good and bad behavior. Direct contact from the boss is the best form of communication. All communications are generally regarded as fake.

Those with egocentric value systems find satisfaction in one-of-a-kind, dangerous, or individualized jobs, and jobs that require great physical toughness and ability. Many in this group are automatically screened out in the interviewing process, because organizations intentionally try to limit the number of employees with this profile. These are the individuals who become militant and tend to file charges on discrimination whenever possible.

Performance appraisals for this group should be highly individualized and given by the boss on a frequent basis. The concept of six and twelve month reviews has no meaning to these individuals. Established wage rates should leave little to no room for discussion .

These people never feel they are paid enough.

This group has the highest turnover rate of all employees. Benefit programs are of little value to this type of individual because many programs require more time and seniority to get more benefits. They are constantly dissatisfied with the boss, the pay, the job, etc. Many times they will drop out of the workforce until it is time to make more money and then try to reenter.

Value System 4 - Conformists Conformists have the classic work ethic; they are oriented toward duty and loyalty. They have a high regard for the written word, policies, job descriptions and work duties. Consistent rules for everyone and a minimum of favoritism by supervisors are preferred by this group.

In communications, conformists respond to written policy manuals, procedures, and duty lists. Communications can be interpersonal but the *shoulds* and the *oughts* need to be emphasized. These people want to understand the logic as well as the directive so that they can rationalize that everything is as it ought to be.

Selection and placement for conformists can be handled by traditional methods. The workplace as we know it is designed around the value system of conformists. Performance appraisals must be conducted and documented on a timely, regular basis. Opportunity for advancement is distinct from promotion since these individuals rely on management to make these decisions.

Pay and benefits should emphasize good work, longevity and good performance. Pay is viewed as a reward for hard work and they do not understand why individuals who do not work hard receive a pay increase. Benefits are viewed as providing security and should increase with longevity.

Motivation is a response to job responsibility, loyalty and the organizational structure. They respond very well to jobs which permit their strong classic work ethic to be expressed.

It is important to have well-defined and consistently administered programs for employees who hold Value Systems 2, 3, and 4.

Just for a moment think what downsizing and reengineering have done to these three groups of people, who comprise about 65% of the total working population. If we surmise that most of these people are married to individuals with similar value systems, imagine the impact on 65% of our total population.

Value System 5 - Manipulative Manipulators are materialistic in their view of life and work. They love wheeling and dealing, opportunities for advancement, greater income, higher prestige and room to maneuver their career plans to achieve personal goals. Opportunity to move ahead is the best motivator.

Communications are most meaningful when they stress opportunities for advancement, objectives for the organization and the challenges for those willing to work hard to receive the benefits of a socio-economic system. Written rules and procedures are often viewed as a barrier to achieving personal goals. This person will often try to manipulate the outcome of information before it's released to the organization. This type of individual will manipulate facts to fit his or her own situation and then justify it through the *flexible ethics* system.

Selection and placement must provide advancement and increasing income opportunities. This group is most often found in positions of leadership. It could almost be called the managerial value system. Performance appraisals need to be goal oriented. These people will seek feedback often to compare their view of themselves with how the boss perceives their performance. Merit pay is acceptable. Pay is extremely important because it is the means to achieve improved status in a socio-economic world. They can be placed on a base pay system to match that of the type 2, 3 and 4, provided there is an opportunity for more in some fashion.

Benefit programs are not as important to these people. They do respond well to the selection and purchase of benefits programs, such as cafeteria style plans. Money, status and *playing the game* are the primary motivators for this individual.

Value System 6 - Sociocentric This group centers on people as the most important part of society and the organization. Interpersonal relationships, human relations, friendly supervision and harmony are the key factors. Constructive confrontation can be viewed as harmful to the organization and the environment.

Selection and placement are important for this group. They prefer a team atmosphere, eye contact and constant verbal communication. Personal contact with a supervisor who is more of a friend than a boss is important to this group. They may not function well in a highly competitive environment. Performance appraisals should take the form of peer evaluation or a group evaluation without singling out specific individuals. If individual ratings are necessary, then stress human relations as well as productivity.

Pay and benefits are very important. This group would pay everyone the same amount and give everyone the same benefits if it could. Anything else would be viewed as creating a dog-eat-dog environment. Their view on pay and benefits is generally very socialistic.

Motivation comes from social relationships, interpersonal transactions and the egalitarian democratic value. The most powerful motivation tool is getting paid for helping other people. This is the only true team minded value system and only comprises about 10% of the population.

Value System 7 - Existential This is a relatively new group of individuals. This group is motivated more by individualism without the negative influences found in Value System 3 and sometimes in System 5. Communications center around the question "Why?" Printed materials are fine, but this group doesn't take printed material as the final word as someone in System 4 would. This group is willing to engage in tasks and activities of all types as long as the benefit is clear. Pay and benefits are important but only to the extent that they can purchase the freedom and opportunity to be one's own self. It's not the amount, it's how you use the money and benefits. This group is difficult to place within an organization. They need the freedom to act and will turn on and off very quickly depending upon the work environment in which they are placed. Strong, authoritarian supervisors are a definite negative to these individuals. This group views performance appraisal as a self-initiated process and in reviews with the supervisor the written document has no meaning. This group is highly motivated by an environment that offers an opportunity to grow, learn, change, make a contribution, explore new territory, and use creative innovation in problem solving. Flexibility is the key to utilizing these individuals to their maximum potential.

Balancing the Various Value Systems Within each organization there will be a mix of the individuals described above. You don't have to develop programs for each group, but you must consider various forms of team development, management styles and communication systems to reach each group effectively. Strong leaders who are known for their power often incorporate segments of all value systems models into their speeches and writing to ensure that all employees get the proper communication. Remembering that most managers ascribe to System 5, it is critical for managers to understand that if it feels good to you, it probably isn't the right thing for the majority of people in your organization.

Value systems are foundations that must be examined when considering how to change the organization. It is very important to understand the various types of value systems and the corresponding traits when modifications are being planned. Most of the new process system tools on the market today utilize a systematic approach developed by one organization. They often fail to take into consideration the importance of another organizational climate, the gap to be closed, and the desired end result. Because of this, inappropriate communications are used and the system changes do not accommodate the various types of individuals within that organization. You can't implement a change successfully without considering all the current value systems and behaviors, and developing a plan that will send the right message to each group.

The graph on the next page outlines the distribution of the value systems found within an organization along with the general do's and don'ts for each.

Estimated Percentage of U.S. Workforce by Value System

Blue Collar / Clerical

Value System	Change	Percentage
Existential	⇑	5%
Sociocentric	⇑	5%
Manipulative	⇑ ⇑	5%
Conformist	⇑	50%
Egocentric	⇑	10%
Tribalistic	⇓ ⇓	25%

Manager / Professional

Percentage	Change	Value System
25%	⇑	Existential
10%	⇑	Sociocentric
30%	⇓	Manipulative
25%	⇓	Conformist
5%	⇔	Egopcentric
5%	⇔	Tribalistic

Probable direction of change during next ten years:
No change ⇔ Moderate increase ⇑ Significant increase ⇑⇑
Moderate decrease ⇓ Significant decrease ⇓⇓

Do's and Don'ts by Value System

	Communication	Job Design	Management Systems and Procedures	Growth Opportunity	Pay and Benefits
2 Tribalistic	DO pass information through the boss. DON'T depend on the printed word.	DO provide a benevolent, protective, autocratic boss. DON'T impose "planing and controlling" onto "doing."	DO recognize that the boss IS the system. DON'T expect compliance with any other system but the boss.	DO make sure the boss gives guidance for advancement. DON'T require long range career planning.	DO make compensation automatic. DON'T use merit pay or complex benefit programs.
3 Egocentric	DO tell him what's in it for him personally. DON'T use logic or folksy appeals.	DO make him feel super-important and powerful. DON'T fail to keep him busy and under control.	DO explain the consequences of non-compliance. DON'T leave any loopholes.	DO explain the consequences of non-compliance. DON'T leave any loopholes.	DO use piece rates or automatic increases. DON'T defer payment.
4 Conformist	DO use the printed word and stress "shoulds" and "oughts." DON'T be inconsistent or leave out details.	DO write detailed job descriptions and duties. DON'T let him lose sight of the purpose and goal.	DO use formalized "Standard Operating Procedures." DON'T expect any originality or creativity.	DO provide step-by-step career plans. DON'T promote until he feels he has earned it.	DO improve pay and benefits for seniority and loyalty. DON'T use merit pay or competitive bonuses.
5 Manipulative	DO imply personal career advantages. DON'T quote what "the book says."	DO turn work into a "management by objectives" game. DON'T fail to specify the limits and boundaries.	DO leave room for some "wheeling and dealing." DON'T forget to audit occasionally.	DO let him run the corporate maze. DON'T plan his career goals and path for him.	DO tie rewards to achieving objectives. DON'T expect benefits to win loyalty.
6 Sociocentric	DO make people the most important subject. DON'T oversell profits and production.	DO set work up for group interaction. DON'T let "participation"overshadow productivity.	DO humanize the system. DON'T let group consensus block implementation.	DO provide opportunity for exposure to more people. DON'T cause competition with his friends.	DO keep pay rates in line with the group. DON'T try to get performance through money.
7 Existential	DO simply make information available. DON'T quote what "management says."	DO get involvement in problem solving and goal setting. DON'T fail to get clear commitment.	DO provide broad guidelines only. DON'T expect obedience to inflexible systems.	DO provide movement in any direction. DON'T be surprised if he refuses a promotion.	DO put intrinsic job interest ahead of money. DON'T make benefits into "golden handcuffs."

Communication Process: Learning Tolerance and Acceptance

Attempting to analyze and understand each person you interact with is not necessary. It would consume far too much time and energy. But a number of factors in our daily interactions can be used to benefit both ourselves and the people we come in contact with.

In developing interpersonal skills, we are told to seek the similarities between all of us. Our actual tendencies are to seek the differences. Focusing on the differences enables us to perpetuate self-deception and destructive behaviors that assure that we remain distinct individuals. Going one step further, we seek to discredit traits that are different in others to strengthen our belief that we are superior. Again, the power of the ego and dominant behavior require that we do this and threaten to take over our thought process.

Take a moment to replay some discussions you've had with friends, relatives or business associates. When the discussion begins to focus on someone who isn't present, it tends to drift either to the negatives or the positives of that individual. Once the focus has been established, the remaining conversation will stay focused on the negatives or the positives. A shift in the perception of that individual in the future now becomes unlikely. After the discussion ends, you don't actually feel any different about the person, yet you participated in reinforcing the group discussion and opinion.

Here's how that concept is applied. In meetings, I have seen a dominant individual make a statement about someone who was not in the room. Whether that comment was negative or positive other people in the room let their fears take over and they join in the conversation. These people are reacting to a fear of disapproval from the dominant individual. By the time the conversation is over, the individual (not present) has been labeled a borderline performer, or he/she has been elevated to new unrealistic heights. Each person in the room has contributed to a distorted perception of the individual. The perception inevitably leads to negative consequences. Do people do this intentionally? Generally, no. They react out of fear of disapproval from

Mr. Dominance and made themselves look acceptable at another person's expense .

Guideline #1 - Our strength as a group lies in our diversity. Don't try to eliminate diversification.

Guideline #2 - Do not promote yourself by making another look bad. It's a game of self-deception that can harm both of you.

Listening is a strong tool that allows us to make contact with others. I vividly remember one afternoon while I was trimming bushes around my house. It was a beautiful spring day and all three of my children were outside enjoying the weather. My daughter stayed relatively close to my side and talked about many different events that had happened during the week. In the normal parental style I responded politely with an occasional nod or grunt to assure that she thought I was listening. Then she asked me what I was going to be doing in the evenings the next week. I explained to her that I was taking one of her brothers to see B.B. King in concert. She immediately told me how she thought B.B. King was great and how she would like to see the concert as well. I explained that I only had two tickets. A few minutes of silence passed. Then she looked at me and asked, "Who is B.B. King?" I felt sick. She had no interest in seeing B.B. King; she was trying to tell me she wanted to spend more time with me. I had completely missed the message she had tried her best to send me in a discreet manner.

This conversation is no different than most in the workplace. How else could so many plans fail so miserably? Listening is neither an art nor a science. It's a tool that we must practice with constantly if we are to use it effectively. I've been told that in singles bars, the art of looking for the hidden meanings in everything that is said, and in every movement that is made, is refined to a state of perfection. There are books and guides on looking for these hidden messages when it comes to sexual relationships. But where are the guides for our everyday listening skills?

During a staff meeting I attended at one company, an assignment was given in a very direct and simple manner: "Please list your department's priorities and outline what you believe the organization's priorities should be." This message was given by the president to a group of vice presidents. Within two days I found that no two of the seven vice presidents came out of the meeting with the same understanding of what they were to do. In fact, one didn't even remember the instructions. When a group like this is unable to listen and understand what is being expressed, how can we expect the organization to function smoothly?

In another incident the pain on a co-worker's face was quite evident. His son had been injured in a car accident and was currently in intensive care. Our boss asked the co-worker how his son was doing. Part way into the fourth sentence, the boss turned to another individual and began talking about the weather. The boss had done his polite inquiry and shut down listening.

Situations like this are not uncommon. Those who blatantly refuse to listen are easy to spot. They expect the normal greetings. When they ask you how you are doing you can respond, "Lousy" and they will come back with, "That's great!" and proceed with their agendas. I've witnessed this at least once a week and it's generally more prevalent among managers than with any other group.

Guideline # 3 - Listening is a powerful tool. Practice it. You must be able to understand the speaker's intent because it contains more information than the actual words you hear.

Following a mediocre meal in a restaurant, the waiter will ask you how the food was. The automatic response, 99.9% of the time, is "It was fine." It doesn't matter if you didn't like the meal. It doesn't matter if the food was cold or tasted stale. We routinely deliver what we think the other person expects to hear. And then we rationalize our response by telling ourselves that it wouldn't make any difference what we said any way.

Here's another scenario: A friend comes over and asks your advice on purchasing a piece of property. You think the person has misjudged the property and probably shouldn't buy it. Will you state that opinion? Will you ask more questions to find out why he's interested in the property and what factual information he's collected? No. You'll say what he wants to hear, "Looks great."

A co-worker invites you to dinner to meet the potential spouse of his dreams. You accept the invitation. But on meeting the individual you see an immature person, someone pursuing status, someone unable to make rational decisions, someone who can't carry on a discussion about anything but the top ten videos on MTV. When asked for your opinion, will you tell the truth? Eventually you will, but only after the heartbreak and the divorce. Just what keeps us from stating an honest opinion?

Every day, employees are called into the personnel office. They are informed that their performance is poor and that they should look for another job; or if this person is an executive, to "pursue other interests." The reaction is generally one of shock and disbelief. Many times, the personnel file doesn't look bad. There are no apparent problems, at least nothing that is significant. All discussions with superiors have been pleasant. Did they not listen or did their bosses take an easy way out?

People want to be dealt with in a fair and honest manner. People receive bad news all the time and learn to cope with it. Honesty doesn't mean brutality. Honesty can be spoken with compassion and empathy. It's surprisingly easy to be honest once you cross the line.

Question: "What do you think of the land I'm going to buy?" Response: "What are you going to use it for? What kind of information have you collected on it and adjoining properties? I wouldn't buy it because .... But you have to decide if it's right for you."

Question: "What did you think of my new potential spouse?" Answer:"I believe that he/she makes you feel good and that is what is important to you. I found myself uncomfortable with the person because I could not see any deep similarities with you. I want and value your friendship, but you have to make the decision about whether that person is truly right for you in the long run."

Husband upon returning from a strip bar: "Sorry I'm late honey, the guys and I went to Embers Cafe for something to eat after work."

Who are we protecting when we don't give honest answers? Who are we hurting? No one benefits from a conversation where anything less than the truth is spoken. All parties participate in deception and eventually everyone suffers.

Guideline # 4 - Tell the truth with compassion and empathy in all situations. Anything less amounts to deceiving yourself and others.

Most people I know avoid confrontation and arguments. These are viewed as win/lose situations and no one likes to lose. There are several viewpoints to every situation. Yes there are differences and the differences are real. But deciding which is right and wrong is a perception issue.

Guideline # 5 - Disagreement does not mean that there is a right or wrong. It only means that a difference in perception exists.

Families, civic clubs, organizations, and unions all have their own little hierarchies. There are always individuals who rank higher than others." Anyone who truly believes this has a strong and motivating ego. No one person is better than another and no one person is lower than another. We are all truly equal. Our functions may differ. Our abilities may lie in different areas. Our contributions may be in specific fields of knowledge or specific tasks we can perform. These differences however do not make any one person superior to another—only different.

Guideline # 6 - No one is better or worse than anyone else. Each person has a gift of certain skills or knowledge and these are the only real differences between us.

Personality Traits

Our review of the Value Systems as defined by the Center for Value Research revealed the basic values that drive each of us. There is no right or wrong value system, but they are different and distinct. These differences in value systems are exactly what can cause problems when we interact as individuals. Even individuals who share the same value system can have quite different beliefs can act quite different from one another.

Each individual is composed of a complex set of traits that have developed from childhood. As child you displayed certain types of behavioral patterns. Chances are you were born with these. These could be described as your personal basic instincts. Your set is unique, just like your DNA.

As you matured, your parents introduced you to another set of traits. Generally speaking, these are the "ought to" thoughts that you have. Have you ever listened to your internal conversations? "I really ought to call my relatives...I really ought to go to the neighbor's open house...I really ought to go to church this Sunday...I really ought to go along with what everyone else wants to do." These are not the things you want to do; these are the things you feel you must do. These are the expectations you place on yourself and others.

As you became an adult you developed an additional set of traits for regular use in your daily life. These traits come from trial and error, observing others and accumulated experience. As you continue to develop you often return to the behaviors that are most comfortable for you. You identify with this set and eventually begin to polish the same groove, refining them to an exact science. This is the comfort zone you have created for yourself. Moving out of this zone is very difficult because it means shedding all that identity you worked so hard to discover. You are now acting out the role you have defined for yourself.

This set of behavioral patterns is then superimposed on your preferred value system. This combination is one of the reasons that none of us act the same, even though we might appear identical under the scrutiny of a psychologist's battery of tests. The roles you have defined for yourself generally fall into one of five recognizable categories:

The first set of traits can be referred to as *action oriented.* Have you ever noticed that certain individuals always feel they must be in charge? This same group is very impatient, often forceful and generally focuses on negative traits they see in everyone else. Rarely can they work in a true team environment because they are too independent. They will not wait for the group decision process. They are not concerned what anyone else thinks. And the rules and rigid structure of a group setting are far too confining.

This set of characteristics is not necessarily negative; it is simply a behavioral style. When placed in the right work environment, these people can meet very high expectations. Positions that require action-orientation—controlling chaos, saving a floundering organization, completing a series of difficult tasks—are all very comfortable to these individuals. When placed in the wrong work environment, they are disruptive and counter-productive.

A second set of traits belong to individuals who are very democratic. These people are generally running a race for popularity. In a social setting there are always certain people who feel compelled to speak to every person present. Don't you know someone who has to be in every organization they can fit in their schedule? In a work setting, these are the happy individuals who are always acting interested in everyone. These people rarely make a decision on their own because they don't want to upset anyone. For them, a comfortable decision process requires discussion and consensus. Even after the decision is made, these people will modify the decision ever so slightly as objections are heard.

This group is very democratic and flexible in their style. They behave as though nothing bothers them. Disappointments are called challenges. Why? Because to call a situation exactly as you see it might upset someone. So they feel obligated to be positive. More often than not, these individuals are overly optimistic about everything. And they avoid confrontation continually. These individuals are most influenced by the last person they've conversed with. People with these traits tend to gravitate into management positions, politics, sales and other *people contact* positions.

The third group of traits are those individuals who have an insatiable appetite to maintain order. Their desks are spotless. They want complete control over whatever they touch. Everything they get involved in is viewed initially as a negative. They plan for the worst scenario and then control processes to ensure order is maintained and nothing gets out of (their) control. Change is very difficult for these people, because the status quo has been upset. Now they too must change and set up a new set of control mechanisms to address a new environment.

Socially, these people are almost perfect to a point of intimidation. They know all the proper rules, the proper manners, exactly what to wear, exactly what to say and not to say. They are always the most mild mannered individuals at the table. In work, these individuals are last to get on the change wagon. They are concerned about where change is taking them and will not accept it until every detail has been reviewed and analyzed. This group is also very dependable. Remember the "ought to" set of traits? These individuals live out the "ought to" functions. These people can be excellent in some jobs and detrimental in others. They are often found in accounting and other "orderly" occupations.

The fourth group of traits are those who are always asking questions, trying to understand everything that is going on. They are generally quiet individuals, deep thinkers that do not have to put on a show, control anything or lead the charge. But they must understand what is going on in detail and will probe every source that they can think of in order to grasp all details and achieve full understanding.

These people are very good at preparing instructional materials, doing research work and functioning in teaching capacities. They accept nothing at face value until it withstands their scrutiny and test. They do not accept the status quo as a given but rather will analyze and question it to determine what is missing or how it can be improved. These people are also slow to move to change. They have to question every detail of the process and fully understand it before they can move forward.

The fifth group can move between each of the other four sets of traits with little effort. These individuals assess every situation and respond with what they believe to be the appropriate method of operation. In a group setting they don't have to be the leader but they can be. They can move forward unilaterally, or they can become very democratic in their approach. They can be comfortable with chaos all around or they can establish order in a situation. They can accept the information or situation as it is or question it in finite detail. These individuals are highly flexible.

Individuals within the fifth group are not easily recognized. If you ask people about this type of individual you are likely to get a conflicting set of answers. They are described by others in the manner in which others have seen them operate in a given situation. They appear to have multiple personalities and fade in or fade out of the picture at any time. How can they do this? A small percentage of the population that has learned to adapt their behavior to each situation. Their ego is in check. They have no defined territory. They respect the opinions of others through the power of listening. They have no personal greed. They are not concerned about what others may think of them as individuals. They are themselves participants and yet they guide others to better performance through their quiet and powerful presence.

Let's examine how these five personality traits could combine with a conformist value system. If we are discussing an individual who has broken the rules at home or in the workplace, the action oriented individual will be the one who overreacts to the situation. If someone has broken the rules she (or he) will punish immediately without asking questions. She doesn't care what others think; she doesn't care what caused the person to act inappropriately; she only sees that something wrong has occurred and it must be punished.

The individual who is democratic in his traits will not act on the situation immediately. He'll collect input from all sources to ensure there is consensus on the rule. He may even consult the rule-breaker to determine what he thinks should be the appropriate punishment. Once consensus is achieved, this individual will carry out whatever punishment has been agreed upon. However he will modify it just slightly during the process to meet at least one objection from the perpetrator. Remember, whoever has the last contact with the democratic person has the strongest influence.

The individual with a tendency toward order and control will consult the manual, rule book and any other guideline that exists and perform the prescribed punishment. It's simple, and it maintains order, control and consistency. The people who try to understand every detail may never get to the point of taking action. They will question the individual about his or her motivation. The questioning will be extensive and almost never ending. After they talk to the individual, they will question others who have had to determine punishment. They will question individuals who have performed the same act if one is available. They will ask others for opinions on the right thing to do. The process goes on and on. By the time a person with this personality trait has completed the process and determined what action to take, many others will have forgotten what rule was broken to begin with.

The individuals who can shift between traits will first talk to the individual. They will question the individual for a short time to determine why he did what he did and how he feels about having done it. If the action only hurt the rule breaker, the fifth personality group will generally take little or no action. Instead, they will work the person into a position that requires a commitment to change the offending behavior. If the action damaged property, they will determine how the individual should make restitution, and what additional punishment should be invoked. If the action involved injury to another person this personality trait will consider the circumstances. If the situation was unintentional, such as a car sliding on ice and bumping into another car and injuring the driver, this personality will limit the action on the individual. If the rule breaker was driving drunk and killed someone, they will recommend life imprisonment or the death penalty. This personality type works to ensure that the punishment is appropriate for the circumstances and within reason of the written rules.

These traits often determine whether we are satisfied in a setting or if we are uncomfortable and dissatisfied. These traits represent basic values that were introduced to us at very early and impressionable times. The way we see the world and how we feel it should be structured is based in our value system. The manner in which we respond to our settings is demonstrated in the personality traits that each of us prefer to use. With all the possible combinations of value systems and behavioral traits, no wonder communication is the single most problematic area in most organizations and most individuals' lives.

There is a distinct formula here. Unless our values, needs, and individual expectations are met, we're not going to respond in a productive manner. Several tools can be used to determine individual needs and expectations. Using these tools in small group settings can identify barriers and explain communication conflicts in a non-confrontational manner. Then both can be dealt with effectively. But until the organization and the individuals are willing to address an issue, the same problems will continue to crop up in daily activities.

Most of us get frustrated with the behavior of others. Explaining why the differences exist doesn't resolve anything, but it can provide valuable insight. It can cause people to learn and grow with new understanding. The messages communicated will develop with greater understanding of others. With increased understanding comes an appreciation of the value of these various traits. No single set is right or wrong. They just exist. People must strive to become non-judgmental of the other styles and learn how they are effective in various settings.

Understanding Team Dynamics

We hear a lot of information about *self-directed work teams* in today's popular media. Many of these teams are ineffective. The truly effective work team, whether it consists of one person or a group, is a *self-disciplined* work team. I prefer to call these self-disciplined groups *accountability teams.* Through the development of self-discipline, tolerance, and acceptance in a self-defined work setting, the stage is set for success.

Certain issues must be kept in mind continually to achieve effective team development:

- The team will never function well if fear is present in the organization. Employees will be reluctant to take the lead.
- Any systems or changes that are implemented must have a mechanism in placc to prevent the good systems of today from becoming the road blocks of tomorrow.

Take a moment to remember the assortment of personality traits and value systems in the workplace. Now you can begin to understand why so many efforts aimed at developing work groups based on traditional team concepts have failed. If your team leader is a manipulator who happens to have the personality traits of a control person, how much participation will take place? The team will act quickly to make a decision and implement it. Whether the decision is right is determined and/or manipulated by the leader. Then the team leader will wonder why there's no support for the program in the organization. The team leader also wonders why the other individuals don't want to participate on the team any longer.

A number of guidelines need to be considered before team development can be implemented:

- Does a team have to incorporate more than one member?
- Is the team going to be responsible for a task or a process?
- What level of research and problem solving activities must be undertaken?
- What time frame has the team been given to accomplish the task or institute the process?
- In what type of environment does the team have to operate?
- Is the team temporary or permanent?
- What exact work process is the team assigned to accomplish?

In addition, you should understand exactly what happens when a team is formed. Often, the process begins with a painful learning and growing period. The team will go through several stages of development. And it must pass through each of these steps successfully if it is to succeed. We will examine each of these steps to identify where teams commonly fail and what can be done to prevent their failure.

Step #1- Determine whether the team is a task or process team.

Most organizations start teams without considering whether the end result is a task or a process. This is important in determining team structure and norms.

Task-oriented teams need to be staffed with results-oriented individuals. The individuals need to be highly focused on an end result, operate independently, and have a sense of urgency. This type of team should include as few team members as possible—three maximum. Team members can always call in others as resources if necessary. But don't encumber the team with too many people. This always slows down the process of completing the task. The number of norms are minimal and structure is not as important here as with process teams.

Process-oriented teams are normally formed to foster changes that will eventually affect the culture of the organization. Their attention is centered on changing a particular method of doing business. In this case, the team must be larger but still limited. Generally four to six members is sufficient. Process team members should be cross-functional in their representation of the organization. The team must include a cross-section of personality types as well.

If your organization is developing this type of team, consider what they are being asked to do. Then select the individuals according to the subject and relative to their impact on the process. For example, if you are forming a team to change the process of distribution systems, you may want to include an individual from distribution (he or she will have to live with the process), someone from finance (to evaluate the economic impact), someone from the manufacturing operation (he or she has to deliver products via the system) and someone from sales (he or she has to ensure the changes don't have a negative customer impact). This is a simple example. *It is not necessary for the team to include management personnel. In some cases it may be better if managers and supervisors are not involved because they are often biased and influenced by those old barriers, sacred cows and unwritten rules. Let employees provide the daily leadership. The supervisors and managers should act as consultants, guides and facilitators..*

Step #2 - Determine the level of research and the type of information that will be needed.

Too often a team is formed without considering the type of information and research that will be required. Many times the necessary information is very difficult to locate internally and must be gathered from sources outside the organization. If you think the team will need this type of information make sure there is a person who can tap into these resources. When a team is unable to go outside of the organization on its own, a barrier crops up and there's a ready-made excuse for failure.

If the information is highly confidential you must share it with the team. If your organization is unwilling to do this, then don't form the team. To protect information you could place only managers on the team but don't expect ownership when the final product is rolled out and passed on to those who are responsible for making it work. *You must be willing to share all the information that is needed for the team to perform its function.*

Step # 3 - Determine the time frame for task completion or process implementation.

If you are looking for quick results from a task-oriented team, keep the team very small, appoint a specific leader, and provide predetermined ground rules for team start-up. Be very specific and don't compromise. The individuals selected must be the type who can make decisions independently and are not afraid to act fast on partial information. Keep in mind that most decisions can be made with 80% of the facts, so don't put anyone on the team who is detail-oriented.

You will be making a mistake if you ask a process-oriented team to get on the fast track. Process involves cultural change. This can't happen overnight. In rare instances it is better to develop a task team to determine the solution and then develop a process team to analyze the solution and implement the process. It takes two different types of individuals to complete process and task. You'll need to separate the problem solvers and the implementors.

Step # 4 - Determine the environment in which the team must operate and be honest about it!

Have you been asked to participate on a team? I have. Then during the first half hour we were presented with everything we couldn't do, along with a general outline of the final results. What is the point of forming a team like this? It's much more honest and far more productive to assemble the group, state what they have been asked to do, and give the instructions. Don't insult their intelligence and self worth by providing all the rules and the end result, and then ask them to be creative. That's like hiring an interior designer and telling her exactly what you want and where to buy it, with instructions not to deviate from your decision.

Today's organization are riddled with sacred cows, unwritten rules, uncontrolled egos, fear, dominance, and territorialism. If you tell the team they have the freedom to operate, then mean it and deliver on your promise. If the team doesn't have the freedom to operate, then question why you are forming one. If you elect to proceed, explain the ground rules but don't expect creative results. As long as the old rules and mores prevail you can't expect new things to happen.

Step # 5 - Determine whether the team is temporary or permanent.

If the team is being developed for a single purpose the members need to be informed up front. This sets a clear expectation of their mission. Participants on a temporary team should be task-oriented individuals.

If the team will be ongoing (i.e. maintenance cost reduction, distribution cost reduction, customer service) then consider the team structure carefully. The most successful method I can suggest is to select a team leader, and ask the leader to select a team based on the assignment. This enables the team leader to exercise discretion in selecting task- or process-oriented people and rotating members as the assignment evolves. This allows more people to participate in the team process over time and designates one individual as the person accountable for ensuring success. *Accountability teams offer considerable flexibility and allow the employees the opportunity to lead and prioritize.*

Step # 6 - Identify the "gap" and use survey data.

When it's time for the team to begin, they need to identify the exact components of their project. Ideally, each team member will be trained in *root cause analysis,* or a facilitator should walk the team through this process. This enables the team to identify key causes to problems in the organization. The benefit of root cause analysis is that it can be used on each problem in the organization. You don't need any other form of analysis if you can perform this one correctly.

You need to conduct surveys within the organization, customer base or wherever else you believe that a problem may exist. Surveys allow for anonymous responses and the collection of clear statistical data. This data will help establish the baseline needed to graph the team's progress. Surveys are extremely important. If the proper ones are used, the data is very reliable.

The next step is to develop a two-axis graph that will list the sequential steps to be taken, the timing of the steps, and who is responsible for the ensuring each step is completed. On the graph's horizontal axis, a baseline should be established. This is a measurement of where your organization is today and an identification of the symptoms you are experiencing.

Upon completion of the root cause analysis, you will have identified the corrective actions necessary to solve the problems. Plot these corrective actions in sequential order from bottom to top on the vertical axis of the graph. You now can draw a line that identifies the gap between today's reality and the goal of tomorrow. The graph contains all the primary information that most employees will want to know: what is going to be addressed, when it will be addressed, which symptom(s) should be eliminated, the time required, and who is responsible.

One graph for each problem keeps the information clear. Posting the graphs in a communications center will keep employees informed of the progress.

Changing from Self-Directed to Self-Disciplined

Panic. Apprehension. Distrust. These are common internal reactions from team members. When you consider all the possible combinations of value systems and personality traits, there are many variables to address in team formation. If these are not taken into consideration, and the team includes both management and employees, then the process will generally follow the three phases described below. I am not suggesting that managers and employees should never be on the same team. Just recognize the difference in personality traits and value systems. It takes time to develop a balance.

The first phase is generally characterized by fear and mistrust. In addition, each person has the option of bringing a hidden agenda, and doubts that the group can really function. They often view the experience as another one of management's time wasters—a cosmetic device to convince upper management that they're doing the right thing. Little is accomplished early in the process. And if anyone in a perceived leadership role (management or union) is part of the team, you can expect to see some territorialism and competitive behavior.

Over the years I've been asked to participate on a number of teams. And because I was a VP, it was often automatically assumed that I would take the lead role. To complicate the process, if there was a union officer on the committee, there was an immediate clash as to what the company could and could not do. It does not matter where the concept of authority lies, do not allow the perception of it on any teams if the teams are to succeed.

The second phase of team development is when the pressure builds. The group generally stops concentrating on the objective and tasks at hand because they are distracted by turf wars and competition. Little has been accomplished as the team focuses more on who is to blame and past sins of the organization. Egos soar, territory is defended and the group makes short term decisions just to get the project over.

The final outcome is the third phase. The final product is generally a compromise between members. The compromises are the result of hidden agendas, lack of trust, ego, territorialism, dominance, and/or an improper combination of team members. The disappointing outcome serves to reinforce that things can't change and now relationships are broken. Managers sell the outcome as positive and those who have to live with the results know the truth.

In building a team, you must be patient and tolerant. Accept the fact that the teams will never do things just like you would. Try to disregard your filters, and learn to listen and be tolerant. Then you will appreciate the creativity that the teams are actually generating.

Selecting the Team Members Remember that not everyone is right for every team. The organizations I have worked in seemed to forget this simple rule. It was not uncommon to see a core group of popular employees who were on all the teams, and a vast number of employees who were never involved even though they were qualified through their knowledge of the subject. As discussed earlier in this section, it's a good idea to define the team and its purpose first, and then select the members carefully. Always recognize that as you place more restrictions on a team, you reduce its chance of success.

Some people will be upset that your work is better than theirs and others will be upset if your work is not as good as theirs. Listen to their comments, but only after you have satisfied yourself. Team dynamics are a lot like nature: everything is interdependent and yet each work piece is dependently originated. Your work will be developed by you, but only with the assistance of others. At the same time the final product depends on the work of all the team members. This is what makes the selection process so critical. If there are several people who think alike, the final product will be narrow in focus. Too much or too little of anything is a detriment, just like water. You need the proper balance.

Selecting the Operating Guidelines A team begins to operate first by establishing some basic guidelines of its own. It's a good idea to bring in a facilitator who is not on the team to help it develop initial guidelines. These guidelines can be simple, such as:

- Deciding the time and duration of the meetings
- Determining how to handle disagreements
- Defining the mission
- Determining the "customers" of the outcome
- Determining that everything to be said will be stated in the meeting (no politicking outside the meeting)
- Deciding how information will be shared within the group
- Deciding whether the group shares credit or blame equally
- Discouraging personal attacks on team members

Remember to keep guidelines to a minimum, and focus on interaction and behavior. Ask each person on the team to share a little bit about themselves with the other members. Position does not matter as much as individual preferences and aversions to details, research, and so on. This gives everyone an opportunity to understand each others' strengths and weaknesses. Once this is completed, the leadership team can proceed with full authority.

As the team begins to operate, trust and relationships will build, honesty in communication will develop and the team's productivity—both individually and as a working unit—will improve. The final product will not be compromised.

The steps to successful team development can be summarized in the following manner:

Face reality. The environment must be right or there can only be failure. If management behavior and restrictions are burdensome don't bother with a team concept until that problem is corrected.

Give the team full authority to act. One of the most destructive threats to a team is limited power to act. Give the team the power to do what is necessary. If management must have guidelines, keep them simple, such as final approval of the plan before implementation.

Instill the desire to take charge. Inspire the self confidence of team members by having the team leader act only as a guide. Often the members must be inspired to take a leadership role.

Set clear expectations. Be concise.

Focus the team. The team must learn to identify root causes of problems, not just the symptoms. They must look at both the tangible and intangible outcomes of their decisions.

Analyze human assets. Know who is being selected for what type of team and why each person is a good choice.

Let the team members define roles and responsibilities. They need to understand each other's strengths and weaknesses and use these to the team's advantage.

Focus on the process during the meeting. Good processes during the meetings are critical to the team's success. Participation, listening, and non-judgmental behavior will all have a positive impact. If this becomes a problem, stop the team, bring in a facilitator and set new norms.

The development of leadership teams within an organization can be quite successful, provided that management establishes a supportive environment for the process. Setting up the teams is not difficult if you follow the simple guidelines outlined above. In fact, the real power of the organization is in its ability to work successfully in productive teams. It's a direct reflection of trust and honesty between the management and the employees. If you are unable to develop highly productive teams, refer to earlier passages on personal behavior patterns. Destructive behaviors must be eliminated before teams can function effectively.

Using Consultants

Consultants are a very interesting group of individuals. This rapidly growing field includes a wide variety of personality types. My experience with consultants has been mixed. Experienced, competent consultants can be of great value in getting an organization over what appears to be a major hurdle.

Employees can see the value in using consultants when their roles are clearly defined and when they are not viewed as threats to the contributions made within the organization. However, more often than not, the consultant is hired to assist management in a non-specific way. This can easily lead to confusion and frustration within the organization. As an example, management may decide that the company's supervisors need training. Many consultants will bid on the training project, specifying what services will be provided and what management can expect to be achieved. A few (good) consultants will ask instead, "Trained to do what? What are the expectations of management? Why do you believe this training is necessary? Is there another root cause for the problems you're experiencing?" *If management cannot specifically answer these questions, then the consultant is being misused within the organization.*

Management, not the consultant, must maintain control of the objectives. The consultant should assist. When employees see the consultant as having more credibility and freedom to act than employees are allowed, the consultant's credibility is damaged and the respect for management diminishes.

I witnessed a situation where management put minimal effort into the initial drafts of the strategic plan because they knew that the CEO's consultant would play the Monday-morning-quarterback-game. They knew the plan would be written a second time reflecting the consultant's ideas and then the CEO would be happy. When upper divisional management responds to the CEO's use of a consultant in this manner, how would you expect employees to respond to the use of consultants by department managers? The most dangerous—and lucrative—consulting alignment is the consultant who is the CEO's "yes person." This assignment is cloaked in tasks, but the objective is for the consultant to tell the CEO that he or she is doing the right thing superbly. This lack of self confidence within the CEO can create rampant problems in an organization. The CEO's lack of confidence coupled with the consultant's "yes" mentality leaves marks of destruction, interference and territorialism on every process within the company. Unfortunately, it is not unusual to see consultants in this capacity. And the only way to regain control is by confronting the CEO.

To use a consultant effectively, I suggest that managers walk through a series of steps to determine the type of consultant an organization really needs.

Here are some basic ground rules.

Know what the consultant is needed to perform. When you first talk to a consultant about a project, he or she should ask immediately why your organization wants to do the project. Your company's definition and the consultant's definition of what needs to happen will probably be different. If you call him and ask for a training program, you should hear three questions:

"Train them to do what?"
"What method did you use to determine the root cause of the problem and identify that this is what you need?"
"What result do you expect from this training?"

Quite often management, as the purchaser of these services, has not determined the root cause of the problem and jumps to the wrong conclusion about what is needed. For example, I once saw consultants hired to train supervisors to motivate employees—but on further analysis it was discovered that training was not what the firm really needed. The company had been hiring the wrong people to begin with. It turned out to be the recruiting process that needed attention. Furthermore, the supervisors didn't have the tools they needed to perform their jobs. And finally, management interference in the work process had put employees in constant fear for retribution for making independent decisions. Consequently, nothing got done without management's blessing each step of the way. Did the supervisors need training in motivation? Hardly. Management needed to restructure the work environment so the employees could perform their jobs.

It's crucial to complete this type of analysis before hiring a consultant. Without it, the consultant can be brought in for all the wrong reasons. Root cause analysis will lead you to the real reasons for system failure rather than the superficial symptoms.

Know whether the work is a task or a process. Task work, such as the design of an employee handbook, is quite concise. If your organization needs an employee handbook, a good consultant can write one with minimal disruption to the organization. The final project can be turned over to the appropriate individual for final printing, dissemination and training. It's a relatively simple process. Most of the task work is direct and easily understood.

Process work is an entirely different matter. Process work normally means that a change is being planned for the organization. To complete this effectively, many individuals within the organization must understand and take ownership in the project from the beginning. A consultant can't do this for you. You can use the consultant to facilitate various components of the project, but he or she cannot make the project work. That's your responsibility. If the work you have in mind is process-oriented, use the consultant *only for facilitation* in:

- Determining what needs to be changed
- How it will occur
- Developing the components of the new system

If a consultant tells you that he/she can introduce the change process for you, don't believe it. The consultant's introduction will amount to a quick training session and then he/she will be gone.

Require performance to a set contract. Many organizations hire consultants to do something without a signed agreement. This is a mistake because the consultant can easily claim that your initial instructions were never clear. Don't hire any consultant until you have the same components of performance and protection that you would require in hiring your auditing firm or a general contractor. When in doubt, add details to the contract and require everything, including a change of scope, to be put in writing.

Talk to your employees first. The solution to your problems is often right in front of you. It's in the people that you are working with everyday. Hiring a consultant can be a success or a disaster. Many times employee morale—including that of top management—has plunged due to the introduction of a consultant without first discussing the purpose of this action. People often jump to the conclusion that management doesn't trust their judgement, and their productivity and creativity levels begin to drop, slowly but steadily. If you search for the answers internally first, and find none, or if there is no one with the required expertise, then you need a consultant. But hiring one without an internal discussion is a serious mistake.

Review the consultant's credentials carefully in relation to the work you need. A major problem in the selection of a consultant is that management generally looks for someone just like themselves. There is also a mistaken belief that the more degrees an individual has, the better their performance will be as a consultant. There is no correlation between the performance of a consultant and the number of degrees he's earned.

If you are hiring consultants to work on the development of a new product in the field of medicine, you do need people with the appropriate degrees. You can't expect an accounting specialist to participate in the development of a new medication or production process.

If you are beginning a project to improve employee morale, the type of credentials required will be quite different. Most managers look for individuals with strong college degrees, but it may be more appropriate to hire an ex-union organizer who was successful in organizing employees. Why? This kind of consultant has been on the shop floor, he can get in touch with the mood and problems of the people very rapidly. His suggestions will likely be simple and much more effective. The consultant with a PhD who has never worked on the shop floor will give you theory and philosophy. The PhD probably hasn't had to implement this type of project or been held accountable for its ongoing results. Remember that in many instances, a consultant's work experience is much more important than a degree. The project will determine what is appropriate.

What additional services are provided? I've seen several consultants come and go through my little community. One of the consultants who earns the most income also has the least repeat business. This gentleman has a PhD and portrays every management trait you could ask for, including excellent marketing and presentation skills. But this person has no work experience or process to follow up the services he's provided. He also charges his clients by the hour, including the follow up calls after the project is completed.

If a consultant is going to bill you like an attorney would, avoid him. This person's focus is to get in and get out, earning the maximum amount of money. There is no emphasis on customer satisfaction and building a long term partnership.

If the consultant has no practical work experience, steer clear. Claiming to be highly educated in a field is quite different from being held accountable for results in the same field. Find someone who has done the work and done it successfully.

If the consultant's proposal doesn't include a follow-up method (i.e. quarterly via telephone, or an ongoing process for an appropriate period) keep looking. He/she should demonstrate an interest in the project's success right from the beginning.

Watch out for the CEO's consultant. Nearly every CEO has a high priced consultant on the payroll. This is the executive "yes" man. This individual's main function is to ask a few probing questions and then tell the CEO that he/she is using good judgement. These consultants don't consider their impact on the organization, the employees, the culture, or any other important factors. What they do take into account is their own relationship with the CEO and how to foster that relationship. When the CEO sends this consultant into the organization, he/she generally lifts ideas from others, visualizes problems where they don't exist, and assesses information inaccurately. This type of consultant does a good job of feeding the CEO's ego, but can be very damaging to the organization. Why does this continue? Because the egos of the CEO (Chief Ego Officer) and consultant feed one another. You will notice that neither of them is ever wrong, regardless of the decision or the outcome, but they can always find reasons and people to blame when projects fail.

STEP THREE:

Communication Methods

A Refreshing Change:
Providing the Information Everyone Needs to Perform

Communication is one of the single most difficult words to define. It means many things to many people. Every organization that I've been associated with has had a communication problem. The process itself is actually simple, but when communication becomes a problem, it can be very difficult to correct.

People usually think of communication only as verbal, but it's much more complex. When you were a child, the communication process was uncomplicated. If you had a thought you expressed it. If you had a question you asked it. If you had a problem you let everyone know. Then you began the process of socialization.

You learned that telling the truth is not always the best idea. You learned that there are ways to communicate without saying exactly what you mean. As you developed more communication skills you learned about the hidden agenda, hidden meanings and the art of negotiating. But as you learned this process, so did your peers. After a time everyone had developed these skills to some degree. At this point your ability to communicate was tainted. You become trained to look for the hidden meaning in every exchange. The more this process is developed over the years, the more complex it becomes.

Then you began to learn about the communication that takes place in the manner people walk, make eye contact and move about during a conversation-the body language era. Books and classes can explain the connection between one's body movements and state of mind. Now the process of communication has become even more complex. Not only did you have to look for the hidden meaning, you had to analyze the body language too.

To complicate the process even more, each of us began to develop our own ego, and defined our territory. At this point we began to filter the incoming communications to protect us from hearing messages that didn't agree with the perceptions we had created for ourselves. It's no wonder communications have been so difficult to correct. We are trying to communicate with one another through layer upon layer of filters. Very little of the real message is actually sent, even less is received and even less is actually understood as it was intended. We have all shared in the development and perpetuation of this process. And it's very difficult to unlearn these habits.

Earlier I recounted the story of my daughter asking to go with me to see B.B. King. She is only 11 years old and already learning the process. Remember the group of VPs who each had a different understanding of a simple project? Managers at this level are masters of the filtration process, a fact that is crippling to the organization. Can you imagine what these individuals must be like at home?

To communicate effectively today you have several factors to overcome. Listening can create an atmosphere of understanding that can be:

- Literal or non-literal
- Intended or unintended
- Assumed general in nature, or specific

For example, the question might be, "'What are you doing for lunch?" How many interpretations can you give that question? "We really need to do something about that group of low performers." What does that actually mean? The list goes on. And the unfortunate outcome is that people are wasting tremendous energy trying to understand the communications within organizations, families, the political system and social events.

Here are some suggestions for breaking down barriers in communication. Before proceeding with this summary I strongly suggest that you review the sections related to ego, territory and dominance. These personal forces are working against each of us every day. These are the forces that will distort the information that you are reading at this time.

The interesting thing is that as the self-deception barriers are built, our world becomes smaller. We become more important in that smaller and smaller world until eventually we're the entire core. It is like entering deeper and deeper into a cave. The more you think of yourself and protect yourself through deception, the darker the world becomes and the more detached you are to reality. As you learn to break down these barriers, the world becomes larger, one step at a time. More light begins to come into view and your vision of reality becomes clearer with the release of each barrier.

People will notice changes occurring within you. I remember one conversation I had with a senior executive involved in personnel. We were discussing what I wanted to do within the organization long term. In fact I had discussed whether there was an appropriate place for me within the organization. We sat for over two hours discussing my thoughts about the future and where I would fit and not fit. His response was interesting and typical. First, he only repeated those parts of the conversation that he wanted to hear, and the ones that fit what he had already formulated in his own mind. Second, the message that he delivered to other senior executives was not what I had stated, but his perception of what should be considered. I had given 100% honest answers that could later be used against me. Following the conversation I wrote a prediction of the final outcome including timetables. I was over 95% accurate. I could see all of his filters operating, and his maneuvers to retain his dominance were in fine form. Had he been honest in the discussion, the result may not have been different, but the process of getting there would have taken less than four months.

Personal Communications

Listening is the first powerful tool we have. Learn to be quiet when others speak. In Native American tribes children were taught the power of listening through the use of a talking stick. When a person held the talking stick, he or she was the only one allowed to speak. All others listened to what the individual had to say and then could ask questions on what had been stated in order to ensure that the message they heard was accurate. No one else was allowed to speak until the talking stick was passed to them. This was an effective means of learning listening skills.

Learning to be quiet includes not only stopping the mouth, but more importantly, quieting the mind. How often have you realized that you've been thinking of something else and missed the last few sentences of a conversation? How often does someone begin a conversation and while he is still talking, you are determining what you will say next? You are successfully blocking the information coming to you.

Never analyze partial statements. In our zest to claim our understanding we often formulate opinions of what is being stated before the message has been completed. Never analyze information until you are sure it's complete and you are certain of exactly what information has been communicated. I'm sure you've heard the phrase "jumping to conclusions." If you are guilty of this, you are analyzing information before the full message is stated and understood.

You can easily recognize those who aren't listening, whether at home, work or in social settings. They turn everyone else into the listener when the current speaker takes a breath. These are the same people who play the game of one-upmanship. As one individual tells a story about a fish he caught, this person must be the next to talk about the larger fish. Generally the non-listeners are the most talkative people in any setting. They don't have time to listen to others; they are too busy listening to themselves and preparing for the next point of interruption to arrive. These people are conducting several destructive behaviors at once. First, they are not getting the message from other people. Second, they are not contributing anything to the conversation other than feeding their egos. Third, they are offending others by rude behavior. Fourth, they are losing the respect of those around them. Fifth, when a clear message is sent, they are unable to respond appropriately. Watch for these behaviors in yourself and others. Everyone does this to a point. We all need to work on these skills.

You can never take back a spoken statement. Once you have spoken, the message is out there. The statement you have made cannot be taken back. You may try to explain it away, but the effect is permanent. The power of the spoken word carries extreme importance. Children do not understand humor from an adult's perspective. Comments about clothing and hairstyle are direct hits on self esteem and ego. Even adults, with all their training and sophistication, are quickly damaged by the spoken word.

Our language is complex. There are very few words that have only one meaning. Look in any dictionary and select just a few words. Aside from the meanings given to words in the dictionary, slang meanings are also associated with certain words. To further complicate communication, each word can carry a personal connotation, either positive or negative, depending on who hears it. In some conversations the speaker and the listener assign totally different values to the same spoken words. Ask a group of people what they hear when you mention the word *spirituality.* The response will vary from laughter, to reverence, to religious views, to opinions of Native American cultures. Ask a group of people to respond to the name *Nixon* or *Bobbitt.* Responses will vary widely.

You need to understand your audience and how they will respond to different words.

Never doubt yourself in a conversation. As individuals we give up a tremendous amount of energy and ability through self recrimination—all that negative talk going on in our minds about how we have failed. During a conversation we all have the tendency to let the other person take power from our own strength and abilities by thinking that someone else is right and we are wrong. Remember, there are differences in opinions and perceptions but there is never a right or a wrong. Don't sacrifice your personal power or freedom by doubting yourself due to others' statements. At the same time be open and practice your listening skills. Every conversation is an expression of ideas and each of us can learn from these ideas, even if it's only to learn another person's point of view.

Organizational Communications

It is very easy to understand why there is never enough communication in an organization, and why so much of it is generally misunderstood. By the time the messages pass through all the organization's filters and personal interpretations the situation is worse than when children play telephone. Productivity and morale are the constant victims of poor communication. Several effective methods can be used to clarify communications, but it's advisable to use a combination of these. Choosing one will not work. Keep in mind that you are trying to get through all the filters and interpretations so that everyone gets the same information at the same time. You will be amazed at the results.

Communication Method # 1 - Large Group Meetings
Employee meetings are not a new idea, but they need to be handled more effectively. I have observed many employee meetings and rarely do the employees benefit. The meetings typically took one of two routes: either management had an opportunity to listen to themselves talk to one another in their own terminology, or it would degenerate into

a confrontation dominated by one or two employees and the top ranking manager at the meeting. Neither scenario supports successful communication.

In any organization there is (at least) a quarterly Board of Directors meeting and a monthly senior management meeting. My first suggestion is to schedule meetings with groups of employees with the same frequency as the most senior management or board. These are your Quarterly Employee Business meetings. In this setting the management of the company can briefly describe how the company is doing. They should not talk about business plans, or use business phrases. The presentations should be brief and directed at specific targets, such as plans for construction, new customers, lost customers, new machinery ordered, and so on. Language should be simple enough for an eighth grade class to understand. The vast majority of the organization does not understand terms such as net vs. gross profits, molecular structures, and strategic positioning. They do understand what will affect them and what they can have an effect upon. Within this meeting include at least one employee speaker to describe what is going on in his or her part of the organization. Have a salesperson talk about what customers are saying about the product and what changes may be needed to improve the company's ability to compete. Ask an engineer to explain a planned expansion. Keep the topics on items that people can understand and influence.

Once you begin these meetings, do not vary from the schedule. If you do, it sends the message that communication to employees carries less priority than communication with upper management.

Communication Method # 2 - Small Group Meetings

These types of meetings should rarely exceed more than 10-15 employees at a time. If your organization has only 20 employees take groups of three or four at a time. In this meeting do not set an agenda. Schedule it over breakfast, lunch, or a snack after normal working hours. Let the employees set the agenda, not management. These meetings are for the employees to ask questions and get straight answers from someone above their immediate supervisors. Take copious notes to ensure that each person's questions are addressed in a timely manner if you can't answer the question at that time.

These meetings can work very well. Unfortunately sometimes the person running the meeting uses it to his personal advantage. In one example the president of an organization held these meetings monthly. Initially they were very successful. First employees were invited, then they began signing up to attend. Eventually the meetings stopped. Why? First, the president used the meeting to tell his story. The idea of the employee agenda and open discussion drifted to a monologue from the president. As this word spread, attendance dropped, then stopped. Secondly, as employees would express concerns, the president would make haphazard comments like, "That should never have happened" (undermining the managers and supervisors). When he returned to his office he fired out nasty grams to the supervisors of these individuals. He didn't know the whole story, but ordered immediate correction. This fed his ego and reestablished his dominant position, but never helped the employees. And his management team and supervisors dreaded each meeting.

If you are going to try small group meetings, stick to the employees' agenda. Do not promise to rectify personal situations. If you are conducting the meeting, keep notes on your concerns and then meet with the supervisor in that area after the meeting is over. Suggest that the employees talk to the supervisors on their own first.

Communication Method # 3 - Post All Meeting Notes

First select a series of locations that are easily accessible to all the employees within the facility. Then at each location put up a large encased bulletin board. Entitle the bulletin board something like "XYZ Communication Center." This bulletin board should display a copy of the minutes from each meeting that transpired during the week. Change the information weekly. It should be arranged in a clearly defined format so that people can easily recognize topics of interest. Never leave information on this board for longer than a week. List the name and internal phone number of someone who can be contacted for further information on each set of minutes.

Invite at least one employee from outside the group to attend the meeting. It makes everyone realize that there is nothing magical happening in there. It's just other employees trying to tackle problems. When this visitor to the meeting sees the minutes posted, he or she can verify that the information is accurate, building trust and credibility.

Another suggestion: When a group is having a meeting, let others sit in uninvited if they elect to. These individuals experience for themselves what the team is trying to accomplish and the minutes that get posted make more sense.

Communication Method # 4 - The Voice Mail System Most of us do not like talking to tape recordings. But a voice mail system that is designed properly can be an asset. It enables a manager or supervisor to deliver information to a vast number of individuals very quickly. The advantage is that the management and supervisory teams can always be fully informed and the rumor mill is stopped very quickly. Just one additional requirement: The managers and supervisors need to pass the information on to each employee reporting directly to them. Use the voice mail system constantly and nothing will be known by the union leadership first. The supervisors will have the information promptly and will become the information source for the employees.

There is an additional approach I have seen used by one manager. When he received voice mail, he responded by voice mail, but he sent the incoming message back with his response. This gives the sender a chance to listen to how disjointed or concise his message was. It's valuable feedback and very effective in improving your personal verbal communication style.

Communication Method # 5 - Personal Contact Forget the open door policy. The issue is accessibility. Managers should always answer the phone. They should get out periodically and move around aimlessly. They should set a personal goal to meet just one person per week in the organization and learn three things: his or her unique family situation, avocations, and strongest feelings about the company (either positive or negative). The manager will know something about the individual's personal life and may learn something valuable in the work environment.

Managers who do this also gain another perspective. As they make decisions, they remember the names and feel the impact of their decisions on people. I call this putting a heart into an organization.

Communication Method # 6 - Collecting Creative Information Look at the size of your organization. Then consider that each one of these people has certain periodicals they read each month. What would happen if the organization paid for the cost of these periodicals with the stipulation that each employee comes up with at least one idea per month that could benefit the company? Researchers could read about new technology. Maintenance people could read about new methods of eliminating the use of solvents or oils. Sales people could read about new methods of customer service. A tennis player might come in with an idea about an entirely new market. Get the picture? Get everyone involved in the business of creating new business.

Communication is a process whereby you learn to quiet your mind, gather the information appropriately and then feed it back correctly. Remember all the filters, traits and value systems that you are dealing with. Just like they say that love is a universal language, you can learn to transcend the filters and blocks by releasing your claim to territory and power. Instead, develop a system of tools that meet the various needs of the types of people you are dealing with. Also remember that you are human. You too have your own personal needs.

STEP FOUR:

Redefining the Organizational Structure

Changing the Paradigm of Silos

Management Guides and Employee Leadership Teams

Every time I walk into a business, here's what I count on seeing: the cafeteria in the basement, the executive offices on the top floor, personnel and purchasing closest to the door, accounting and data processing taking up the most room and a quiet area for the engineers and research people. Behind all of this is where the action is happening. Has anyone ever thought about the plant being in front? Has anyone thought about locating the executive offices near the center of the building or the cafeteria? How about placing engineering and research functions in the plant?

Organizations are still very departmentalized. Cross-functionality is something everyone talks about but no one wants to fully explore. And why should they? Tradition is broken, territory disappears, people must take ownership for processes rather than functions—sounds uncomfortable! But it is necessary if the organization is to survive.

Organizations have traditionally been structured from the top down. Unfortunately, this type of structure does not deliver lasting results. It doesn't provide a work environment in which employee leadership can develop. And the management guides who can teach and facilitate are typically absent. The motto may be customer focus, but everyone in the organization is focused above themselves, with their backs to the outside world. Employees are practicing survival. Organizational structures today are vertically driven—not process driven with a link between employees and customers. Organizations are financially driven, leaving the people component out of the equation. Organizations are based on hierarchy and authority, with the managers and supervisors always having the last say. This environment suffocates employee leadership, self-discipline, creativity and risk taking. In this type of environment, few employee ideas can survive the political and bureaucratic maze that must be navigated to reach their destination.

Changing the organizational structure is necessary before ideas can flow upward easily within an organization. The roles of employees and managers must change. Leader-guide relationships must replace authoritative hierarchy. Senior management must be disciplined, supportive and fair. Managers and employees draw from different assumptions of motivation and behavior within the same environment in order to accomplish superior performance.

It can be both fun and profitable.

Crumbling the Silos The ancient structure of the organization makes it hard to function. People are specialists by nature. Rarely do they recognize that what they are doing affects others in the organization. Nor do they know how.

We talk about communication and we talk about a *shift to process* but the organizational structure remains constant. The structure itself is one of the main impediments to organizations' progress.

First, we are not encouraging cross-functional training. We encourage specialization. We recognize the concept of internal customers, but rarely does a department or an individual identify who those people are. We talk about the company's vision and goal, but rarely is there a mission statement for each functional group. We talk about people becoming more involved but we provide limiting job descriptions.

Ideally, every person entering an organization should be required to work in at least three different areas before going into the function he or she was hired for. The three areas are (a) the group where his/her work will originate (b) the customer group of his/her future work assignment and (c) the group that he/she will interact with most often.

New employees should learn about the process of the organization first, then learn the specific responsibility that they are to perform. They can witness first hand the problems that are generated by internal suppliers, as well as internal customer problems. They learn where communication can break down. And they can take this knowledge to the new job and make immediate improvements in the work process.

As work flows through the organization, it becomes a long series of tasks rather than a smooth flowing process. Typically, no one sees the end result of his or her efforts. Walk through any corporation and ask people what they do in their jobs. They will give you a list of tasks. Ask them what they are responsible for and they will repeat the list of tasks. Look at their daily planners—they list only tasks. Only a minimal concept of the total process exists.

You need to start from ground zero in redefining the organization. When you chart the work process and the jobs in the organization you will find that the process is in the shadows and white spaces of the organization chart. It's not in the boxes that clearly define a job function as we know it. The boxes may be the blocking points. View the chart as if it were a photographic negative. In other words, the boxes become the white space and the shadows and the white space become the areas to fill in.

Those at the top of the organization chart should take the role of *process guides.* These people should lead because of their total knowledge of the business and their facilitation skills. These are the champions of process. They should be the individuals who are reaching constantly for that five and ten year vision, and reviewing the process to see that it is functioning to achieve the organization's desired goals. These people should be great facilitators.

Directly below these guides should be a second set of guides who link process performance to daily activities. These people are trainers, coaches, and counselors. The next level should be those responsible for the daily functioning of the process. These individuals should be the leaders of each section of the organization. These are the people who make the process happen and have the freedom to get the job done. These are your employee leaders.

You will note I have described only three levels. This type of structure yields a flat organization chart which empowers employees at all levels.

This structure creates a balance between long term vision and process development at the top (management guides focused on continuous improvement), the link between vision and daily activities (consistency in purpose and the use of tools) and maintaining the gains for improved performance (employee leadership).

One major corporation allegedly started its business by making every employee a leader with one function: ensure that the customer is happy and will come back. With the freedom to act and clarity of the mission, no one had any questions about what to do and where to focus. Do you think this is impossible? If so, I don't want to own stock in your organization ten years from now. Guides, facilitators and leaders will make these changes happen—not ego, dominance and territorialism.

It is necessary to change this focus so that a feeling of ownership can be developed by all employees. The organization can be structured into a series of mini profit centers. Measure the performance of these groups against performance of external groups who specialize in the same function. The mini profit centers can be designed for maintenance organizations, personnel departments, accounting departments, data processing, business units based on market or product areas, and more. In this manner people will develop ownership of the products and services they are providing internally. Employee leaders will automatically shift away from non-essential functions. You can escape the cost of reengineering because managers will do what they should have in the first place. Let each employee leader define a standard of excellence for his or her functional unit. They will perform harder to achieve their own goals in a process setting than trying to work towards goals management has set for them in an authoritative silo organization.

Keep in mind that the final organization chart should reflect the processes. Any reflection of a specific specialized group can be detrimental to changing the culture of the organization. People have unlimited insights into improvement, but are not prompted to change under the current structures.

Changing the Recruiting Focus

When people are hired into an organization they are generally placed on probation. What a positive start this signal sends. They end up on probation after going through a rigorous series of interviews and being selected as the best. In addition, we ask questions regarding their specific job skills and let the important questions pass. When they are hired we know they are (for example) expert process engineers but can they act as employee leaders or management guides? Usually we don't know because we never ask whether they are process- or task-oriented. Then we wonder why the individuals don't fit in, even though they can do specific tasks well.

Where should we put the focus when interviewing? After asking the questions about technical competence in a specific area, shift to questions that relate to the organization you are trying to build. There is a science to developing these questions, depending on your organization. Remember that knowledge can be purchased anywhere; but desire, strength and process mentality cannot. You need to select the people who have these capabilities.

Sample questions that you might want to ask:

1. What does quality mean to you?
2. What is the difference between an internal customer and external customer?
3. How should work be determined each day when you arrive on the job?
4. How does effective communication occur?
5. Who's responsibility is it to provide the communication?
6. What do responsibility and accountability mean to you?
7. How should employees' success be measured?
8. What is the difference between process and task?
9. What role should employees play in an organization?
10. What role should the supervisor play?

11. What role should upper management play in the organization?
12. What is the ideal working environment for you?

The list of suggested questions can be endless. It takes only about one dozen carefully worded questions to determine if you have the right person in front of you. If not, keep looking. Remember, that the knowledge can always be purchased through other sources until the right individual is found.

It takes both process- and task-oriented individuals to make an organization work properly. But the organization will be stronger if the process people are inside the organization and the majority of the task-oriented individuals come from consulting or other external sources. Task-oriented individuals can get things done rapidly, but sometimes speed and time are the thieves of creativity. An organization's task masters, if internal to the organization, should be in a facilitation department all its own that can perform both internal and external work.

Don't be afraid of new concepts. If you are hiring people for a specific purpose, and recognize that if they achieve that purpose there may no longer be a job for them, tell them up front. Then offer an intellectual performance bond. When they deliver the results, they have a *golden parachute* until the next opportunity arises elsewhere. Never be selfish in the recruiting process; it will only cost you more in the long term. Recruiting must be viewed as a strategy rather than a task.

Changing the Compensation and Benefit Systems

When the organizational structure changes, the compensation system needs to change as well. Straight hourly rates are no longer effective. Major bonuses for executives will no longer be tolerated. Systems must be designed to reward all employees to the fullest extent.

The first step is to recognize that everyone throughout the organization must be on the same system. No one should be treated differently. Those who resist this concept and argue against it are those with strong ties to ego and territory. They typically have no identity other than the perceived superiority that their job title and extra money bring externally. These are not the leaders of tomorrow nor the guides that are so desperately needed. They are the anchors.

Determining which compensation system is appropriate to your organization is a very broad subject. It depends on what drives the business. Performance in both financial and non-financial areas must be measured. In many cases the long term success of the organization is in non-financial measures because these drive the financial measures. Systems may be based on gain sharing measures, productivity measures or employee attitude surveys. The measures will be decidedly different for leaders than for guides. But they will all be based on the same premise—continuous improvement. And as for the percentage of payout or increase, the payout should always be the same percentage for excellent performers, the same for medium performers or no increase for poor performance. Special slush funds should be developed to reward innovation and creativity—and when it is awarded it should be recognized publicly.

Benefit systems also need to be overhauled. Today we tout the forward vision of cafeteria style programs. The systems of tomorrow will need to take into account much broader options, such as more vacation, more allowance for family issues, more portability.

An example of portability would be in the area of retirement programs. Many companies offer defined benefit plans. Employees receive a retirement figure based on their years of service and an average of earnings. Today people want what they have earned. These types of retirement plans should be thrown out the window in favor of portable dollar amounts in a 401(K) or similar plan. The funds are transferable as the individual changes jobs, the company does not have the burden of unfunded liability and government regulations, and it eliminates the record keeping for individuals who worked at the facility for five years, 30 years ago.

Changing Personal Recognition: The New Form of Performance Assessment

One partially functioning area—the performance appraisal—will need major changes too. Most organizations today use an antiquated system where the supervisor explains his/her perception of the subordinate's performance through the course of a year. The subordinate hears what his/her perceived strengths and perceived weaknesses are. Generally what is really being said by the supervisor is, "Here's how you can be more like me and less like yourself." And it's amazing how many weaknesses people have in a work environment that generally does nothing to unleash the individual's real potential.

The most effective performance review will involve input from all portions of the organization. The performance measurements should be on *total performance* within the organization. To conduct an individual's performance assessment, information is collected from the departments where the work originates, the internal customer base, at least two peers, at least two other individuals of a level above the individual and at least two individuals who report to the person. Information on perceptions, performance, interpersonal communication skills, creativity, facilitation, is collected from each evaluator. The information is then put into a sensible format. How are the positives identified? By customer satisfaction and interpersonal skills. How are the weaknesses identified? By the skills that are not identified as strong and would be important to master to achieve what the individual wants to achieve as a career goal. Included in the feedback is also how well the individual is utilizing the tools the organization has accepted as the norm for process improvements. You then are measuring personal characteristics (task) and process characteristics.

To an extent, the concept of *360-degree feedback* is really collecting the right information from the right sources and ensuring that the individual receives the information with as few filters as possible. Although 360 degree feedback is a new fad term for this process I do not believe that it truly fits. To me, the fad term conveys an image of talking to yourself continually.

The process is simple and effective. It also removes most personal biases, filters of deception, and other misinformation. This allows the individual to set his or her own expectations instead of working toward someone else's.

Striking a Balance in Life

There is a revolution going on today. It is quiet and non-violent. It is also very real. People are not willing to work the excess hours any longer. Employee loyalty is gone. Company loyalty to employees is gone. I hear many employees, whose families have grown, wishing they had the time back to do it over the right way. They complain that they spent too much time at the office and not enough on their families and themselves. There has been an ever increasing shift in our society toward more and more material items, and the expectations of organizations have changed to match this desire.

When you rent a movie you can replay the parts you like the best or the parts that you missed. When you read a book you can reread the parts you don't understand or that you really like. In life you have one opportunity and then it is gone.

The more we develop a take attitude, focusing on external success, the more we give up of ourselves, our families and our lives to maintain our collections. There appears to be a growing imbalance in individuals. It is manifested in many ways—divorce, problem children, alcoholism, lowered self esteem, marital affairs, drug usage and the list goes on. Society loses out as this process occurs. Crime rates are up. Caring goes down. Giving goes down.

Fewer and fewer people are paying the rent back to the communities in which they reside. We get home from work and shut the door on the outside world and often on our own families. We don't allow ourselves simple pleasures any longer. Pleasure is compressed into a short period of time packed with activity and little meaning.

Years ago I can remember using my imagination in games with other children and by myself. Today my children do not have to exercise their imaginations; they just turn on the television. I actually thought they were happier with this existence. It took me almost two years to find out that they were actually more interested in spending time as a family or with me but were afraid to ask—because I was never home but at the office. I've now drawn the line on work. No more weekends. No more continual late evenings. No more missing the activities my kids are involved in. The balance is coming back and I will give up my job before I would give up my balance. If I don't, what will the organization give me in return for this sacrifice? What I discovered is that they have nothing equal to the importance of personal satisfaction and the joy of family strength and relationships. The company can only tolerate it, not plan and encourage it. Organizations that don't support this freedom will be unable to attract quality performers in the future.

My situation is not a unique example. Business magazines are filled with articles about people giving up excellent jobs to have an excellent experience in life instead. New graduates are hard to recruit from many schools. There is an emerging focus on lifestyle and the balance in life. Companies are not ready to deal with this new reality.

Organizations are going to have to plan for this new workforce. More and more talented individuals will be lost from the workplace as they seek this balance. Many organizations will be unable to respond. I can envision employees being hired to work a specific amount of time each year followed by free time to experience their life. Instead of retiring at 55 as I was taught, these people are talking about working until death—but about eight to nine months each year. This allows plenty of time for family, community, self and spouse. I believe that as one of the benefits of the future, the semi-contract employee will become more prevalent as our society begins to recognize the need to regain this balance in life.

SECTION FOUR

Putting It All Together

A Blueprint to Guide the Journey Beyond 2000

Each of us has the power of choice. It is a personal power that no one can take from us; we can only give it away if we choose to. You can make the choice to change the way you live, the choice to help change the imbalance in your life, and the choice to help change an organization into a dynamic place to work.

The power to change is born within you. No one else can make it happen. You must make the choice. The past must be forgotten and the present put aside. The future is where you can live beginning today.

Choices are made first by an individual, then by a group of individuals, then by a family or organization. Eventually, these choices can be spread slowly but consistently. Be patient and persistent.

Choice # 1 - Begin to change yourself.

Each of us is carrying an assortment of mental baggage that clouds our perceptions of the world around us. It is difficult to see clearly through this shroud. You can remove these filters and enrich your total life—in the family and at work. There are a number of methods you can use and should concentrate on. Let's review the effects of ego, territory and dominant behavior on ourselves, those around us and the organization.

The effects on you are slow and deliberate. As you become more and more convinced that you are something you're not, you divert more energy and focus on maintaining this deception. And that is all it really is—a deception. People can get so caught up in who they think they are that they can't exist without their external material collections. They must have titles, they must have power, they must dominate others—all in an effort to maintain the false perception. There isn't one individual who is more important than another anywhere. We all perform different functions, we view each situation differently, we are affected by events in a different manner but that's all that exists—differences, not importance.

The following summary of guidelines will help you initiate a positive change in your behavior:

1. ***Control your ego.*** Recognize that the ego must be controlled or your potential and that of those around you will never be realized. Keep track of the excuses that you use daily and rid yourself of them.

2. ***Eliminate your fears.*** You must confront your fears in order to learn where your potential is being withheld. Write down how you can face these fears. Then do it.

3. ***Stop dominance and territorialism.*** As you see dominant behavior, call it out in the open. The more attention drawn to dominance and territorialism, the sooner the game will stop.

Choice # 2 - Learn to communicate effectively.

In order to begin the change process within yourself and within the world around you, you must learn to communicate effectively, both verbally and in written form. The most powerful tool is your ability to listen and to clear your mind of clutter. Effective listening skills coupled with observation give you tremendous power to communicate with anyone that you meet. It also provides you with an uncanny power that others can't grasp, but they are not afraid of it. You are constantly feeding them with energy that enables others to improve their lives both at home and in the workplace. The rules for effective communication are simple and you can implement them immediately. Let's review the various methods and tools that are available for improving communication.

1. Our strength as a group lies in our diversity. Don't try to eliminate the diversification.

2. Don't make your self right or good by making others look wrong or bad. You are only deceiving yourself and can harm others.

3. Listening is a powerful tool. Practice it. You must be able to understand the intent of what is being stated for it contains more information than the actual words you hear.

4. Tell the truth with compassion and empathy in all situations. Anything less is deception of yourself and others.

5. Disagreement does not mean that there is a right or wrong. It only means that there is a difference.

6. No one is better or worse than anyone else. We each have a gift of a certain set of skills or knowledge to offer and these are the only real differences between us.

Choice # 3 - Begin to use the right tools effectively.

As you implement new tools you can only expect results if you have achieved progress in Choices #1 and #2 above. The tools are nothing more than a process, and help explain what you need to do to improve organizational performance. The tools are only as effective as you allow them to be. Think of all the programs that have been the fad, and failed in hundreds of organizations. Failure of the fads is far more prevalent than success. The reason is simple. Wherever you go, you are still there. This is true of everyone that you meet. Personal change and improvements in communication must take place before the tools can be effective. Otherwise you will be getting the same limited results as in the past. Let's review the tools that are effective in developing employee leadership and management guides.

Changing the Recruiting Process You can buy knowledge anywhere, but hiring people that fit your organization now and where it needs to be in ten years is the difference between success and failure. Recruiting needs to focus on process and environment development and not on the specific skills that a person believes they possess. Refer to the earlier section on the recruiting process. Then keep in mind the following specifics:

- Communication is the first key criteria to look for
- Understanding of quality is the second most important criteria
- Understanding of process vs. task ranks third
- Proper leadership is fourth in line
- Proper understanding of facilitation or 'guiding' is also very important
- Understanding of the destructive forces of ego, dominance and territorialism are essential

The Use of Value Systems The information contributed by the Center for Value Research in Section Three is critical for success. It enables you to identify the value systems of various candidates during the interview and employment process. It enables you to design compensation systems, benefit systems, recruiting methods, performance methods, communication systems, quality process systems and new organizational structures that fit the organization you are creating and yet meets the needs of the types of employees you hire. Proper use creates a strong motivational environment for people to achieve their best performance. Look at the various types of values we have discussed.

The Identification of Traits The people you are working with all have different traits that affect their behavior. These traits are neither good nor bad, just different. You can identify these traits and make them work for both the organization and the individual. You'll no longer be putting people in jobs that are uncomfortable for them as individuals. And you will maximize both your potential and their potential. Review the key aspect of these traits.

The Use of Surveys Surveys are quite powerful. Used properly, they can identify a baseline of your current position and your desired destination. The employees can then develop a process to close the gap. Identification of the gap between today and the future gives you all the identification of change that the organization needs to undertake. Forget what every consultant tells you as they attempt to sell you more and more programs to correct problems that may not even exist. Use surveys to identify the gap and the employees to develop the plan. Management should only act in a capacity to guide and facilitate the process.

Surveys can be completed on virtually any aspect of your organization. Employee attitudes, internal and external customer satisfaction, vendor and supplier performance, etc., can all be measured. Then this information can be used in setting up plans, objectives, and performance assessments.

The Use of the Communication Tools The communication tools that have been identified in this book can be put to use immediately. Once the gap has been identified it can be tracked visually using bulletin boards and on-line computer systems. Then everyone can observe the progress of each of these key areas. Employees are given the information they need on a weekly basis. Aside from tracking the closing of the gap, your supervisors, managers and employees are kept well informed through the posting of meeting minutes and the voice mail system. Review the communication systems identified in this book. Here is a summary of the highlights:

Personal Communications

- Listening is the most powerful tool you have.
- Never analyze partial statements.
- Remember that you can never take back a statement.
- Never doubt yourself in a conversation.

Organizational Communications

- Use large group meetings on a continuing basis.
- Use small group meetings on a continuing basis.
- Post all meeting minutes for everyone to read.
- Use the voice mail system to update people daily.
- Use personal contact with one person per week.
- Use employees as the information gathering system.

Changing the Performance Assessment Process The current methods utilized are antiquated and full of subjectivity, They really do not address issues as they relate to the organization, but rather only as the supervisor sees the situation. By changing the process, you collect interactive feedback that is more focused on the individual's performance within a process environment. Take a moment to review the elements of the new performance assessment method:

- Get feedback from at least two individuals reporting to the person.

- Get feedback from the person's customers.

- Get feedback from the person's suppliers.

- Get feedback from the person's peers.

- Get feedback from two individuals one level above the individual.

- Get feedback from the individual as to what he/she expects not only from the job but his or her needs for a balance within life.

- Structure the summary of the feedback and provide it directly to the individual verbally and in writing.

- Incorporate both personal performance and the use of the process tools and systems.

Changing the Organizational Structure Changing the organizational structure is very key to success. People must be placed in an environment that makes them think about the process rather than about specialized roles. A specialist's focus is too narrow to promote process. Remember, the knowledge can always be purchased. Performance in the organization is what you should be concerned about.

You need to eliminate the silos, create cross-functional departments and develop a series of mini profit centers throughout the organization. Let's review the highlights of the new organizational structure:

- Eliminate functional departments. Then structure around process.

- Create leadership teams throughout the process.

- Eliminate fear in the individual working environment.

- Begin to build trust and confidence between all employees.

- Let the employees provide the daily leadership.

- Managers should provide only facilitation or function as guides.

- Develop extensive cross training programs for all employees.

- Build self discipline in all employees.

Team Development Team development is necessary if people are to become the leaders of the organization. Teams are not large groups of people, nor are they a collection of similar individuals. To develop employee leadership you must take into account the value systems, the traits and the process that is identified. Once this analysis is completed, the teams can be formed and operate freely within the organization. Following is the summary of the key points of team development:

- Determine if the team is to be process- or task-oriented.

- Determine the level of research and the type of information that will be needed.

- Determine the time frame for task completion or process implementation.

- Determine the environment that the team must operate within and be honest about it.

- Determine if the team is to operate on a one time basis or if it will be an ongoing team.

- Identify the gap and use survey data to map the route and track your progress.

- Ensure that the obstacle of fear is not present.

Install systems to ensure that the good programs of today do not become the road blocks of tomorrow.

Choice # 4 - Turning Employees Into Leaders

It's up to each individual to initiate change. But people can't begin to change unless a conducive environment exists. You now have a blueprint to create the environment. You must let go in order for people to excel. Spontaneity will emerge within the organization. Creativity will develop. Remember that creativity is nothing more that taking bits and pieces of something and putting them into a new format. Creativity does not include or operate in an atmosphere of fear, bias or rules. It flourishes in an environment of freedom, release and compassionate understanding.

People will take responsibility and leadership. It is a learned process that develops through facilitation and guidance. When a problem arises, don't rush to solve it yourself. Give it to the team that is accountable and assist them through facilitation to reach a solution. Remember that their result and methods may not be the same as yours, but with the right process the right decision will always emerge.

By turning off the management examples that we believe people learn from, we allow the energy within the employees to develop. It's analogous to turning off the television and asking your children to develop a new game by using their imaginations. Soon it becomes easy.

Choice # 5 - Turning Managers into Guides

For a manager to become a guide the first step is growth in accepting reality. You are no more important to the organization than the newly hired janitor. You are just performing a different function within the organization. Rather than control, managers need to develop unbridled curiosity, seeking experiences and learning rather than collecting names and faces.

Focus on becoming non-judgmental. Your way is not the only way. There are many ways to solve a problem. Your definition of right and wrong is based on your self perception, not on reality. You must recognize that you are not superior or wiser. Focus on changing destructive behaviors.

Once we have defined who we think we are it becomes more and more difficult to allow new information into our lives. We begin to live in a rut and our vision becomes a tunnel that only admits information that makes us feel better about ourselves. When one startling reality hits you, you'll know that you are on the way to recovery: No matter how interesting you think you are, you'll find that you are quite boring when left alone. You are only interesting if you have a captive audience that you can perform for. Think of the clear mind as a blank piece of paper ready to accept new imprints and figures. In real life the mind is a large dissected grid that is cluttered with rules, regulations, culture, myths, ethics, religion, sexuality, work expectations, home expectations, parental expectations, spouse expectations, trust, etc. Is it really any surprise that it's difficult to get new information into this cluttered closet? We spend our time shadow boxing with this grid rather than cleaning it up.

A guide is a content person who continually strives for learning, happiness and experience. A guide gets satisfaction only from giving. If you gain satisfaction only through positive feedback from others you have a long way to go to become a guide. You are a follower that is attempting to act like a leader and probably not being very successful at either. Your credibility comes from within, not outside.

Remember that your biggest enemy is internal. It is what you convince yourself that you are or are not. This internal enemy, although powerful, does not have the ability to regroup as you begin to defeat it. Unlike an enemy of physical war, once it is defeated, it is gone forever. Your internal energy to make these changes is infinite. Unlike external energy that requires constant feeding and nurturing, the internal energy is always present and powerful enough to defeat any enemy you have mentally created for yourself. It is time to step up to the challenge and create the new map of reality for yourself.

Choice # 6 - Creating Balance Within Your Life

Anything that is not used for an extended period of time will begin to atrophy. The longer this process extends, the better the chance that the atrophy will become permanent. It's true of everything in your life.

The longer you fail to communicate and interact with your children, the more difficult it will become to communicate with them. The longer you spend away from nurturing the relationship with your spouse, the more difficult it is to maintain it. The longer you go without dreaming and using your imagination, the more difficult it becomes to awaken it. The longer you live in self-deception, the tougher it is to get out of the trap. The less you give of yourself, the more difficult it becomes.

We have all been raised in a society that is based on consumption and use. We do this with everything we buy and we do it with the people we meet. We have learned how to take and use, and forget how to give and nurture.

More and more people are abandoning conventional styles of living in this society. They are adopting new ideals that incorporate a balance in life that includes family, self, work and community. The changes may not seem apparent at first, but take a closer look.

There is a renewed interest in inner peace. Spirituality is awakening throughout the country. People are turning to eastern philosophies and the ways followed by the Native Americans in a search to find inner peace. There is growing belief in the power of spirituality and its affects on our environment. As I heard a highly respected individual ask one day, "Are we humans who have spiritual experiences near death, or are we spiritual beings who have elected to have a human experience and we begin to sense our true existence when nearing death?"

Everything that exists on the planet is interdependent upon everything else. Ancient cultures understood this. The Native Americans understood this. Today we recognize nothing as interdependent but view ourselves as independent from one another and from nature. This is a fatal deception. And the only way to continue the deception is through continued destruction—of the environment, of each other, and of the opportunity to experience life to its fullest.

Not everyone can or will accept this thought process. But remember one important point if you remember nothing else: you have the power of choice and with this power you can begin to improve your life, your family, your organization and the world in which we live. The choice is truly yours.

Choice # 7 - Adding a New Dimension

Honesty and openness are not weaknesses. Gaining new experience is valuable. Keeping an open mind is essential. We are embedded in our materialistic world and fully equipped with mind filters to maintain our self deception. We miss out on the essence of life and what makes each of us perform to our fullest and enjoy what we have today, now. As mentioned earlier, many ancient civilizations were more in tune with the workings of life than we are today. You need not look far to see that some of the new tools gaining recognition are not new, but a re-awakening of a sleeping force that has always been present. These practices are sometimes called "new age" even though they have existed for thousands of years. Let's look at a few that are being used today.

In ancient civilizations there was a recognized force that was described as "permeating the universe and everything within it." Today it is often called spirituality. Every ancient civilization was immersed in it. Although the rituals surrounding the concept developed differently in different cultures, the basic premise was the same.

As civilization became more *civilized,* spirituality took on a different meaning. It developed into religious forms—rituals that were practiced one day a week rather than a everyday state of consciousness that recognized a spiritual existence. Civilization shifted from living in harmony with the environment and tolerance of others to a materialistic state that entrapped everyone born into this world. It is and continues to be an evolutionary process. But look toward the future. If this evolutionary process continues there are only two options. Complete destruction of the world as we know it due to over consumption, hatred and violence—or a rebalancing of our existence that respects and strives for an integrated and non-destructive existence with the environment and with each other. There is no place for the 60-hour work week and the personal greed that have created so much imbalance in our existence.

This evolutionary process means that what we are experiencing today will not be what we'll see as civilization in the future. And it is my belief that the new future is within our lifetime. Ancient philosophies are reemerging. Hospitals are adding holistic practices as part of their standard medical treatments. Some have gone as far as adding wings for the practice of holistic healing based on ancient practices as an augmentation to the current treatment. Some of the practices that I have seen rising in popularity—for reasons unknown to our black-and-white-prove-it scientific communities—are being reexamined.

Yoga Yoga is an example of an ancient art form founded in spirituality. Individuals have found that by practicing some of the ancient techniques, body strength, mental clarity and health are improved dramatically. Is there a place for this is the business world? Consider the stress placed on employees in a reengineered, downsized organization, or look at the executive who is traveling the world and changing a significant number of time zones daily. Through some simple exercises it has been proven that these individuals can revitalize their energy and begin to relax. Who benefits? Everyone.

Acupuncture Another ancient art is acupuncture. Although laughed at just a few years ago, it is now being covered by some insurance polices as a realistic and effective means of treatment for certain conditions—and more importantly, a means of prevention for many others.

Massage This concept has had a bad connotation. In many people's view, it's either for the red light district or for the extreme sports enthusiast. In fact there are many useful forms such as Reflexology, Shiatsu, Swedish, full body, etc. Each is designed for realignment of what many ancient civilizations referred to as energy fields, and the elimination of toxins within the body. It was not developed as a form of foreplay but as a form of health.

Healing Touch This practice was developed and refined earlier in this century but there are accounts describing it dating back to early Greek times. There now exists a certification process for practicing this therapy. Some physicians are now recommending this treatment to augment conventional treatment. This practice is fully founded in contacting an energy source that permeates the universe and asking for assistance in rebalancing the life forces and energy within the body to help the healing process. Thousands of people will attest that it works. It is also a state of mind. Think of how medical researchers have tested placebos and how often the groups receiving the medication fair no better than those not receiving the treatment. Is it coincidence or the power of the mind?

Meditation Every ancient civilization has practiced meditation for the purposes of relaxation and achieving oneness with an unseen energy. Meditation takes on many forms but the outcome is usually similar—a strong alertness to the world around you, a sense of peace and an ability to accomplish whatever you focus on.

Aromatherapy This practice has been around for centuries, as documented in Egyptian and Japanese cultures. It is currently considered a bonafide medical treatment in Europe. Indians used many forms of aromatherapy in their rituals. Both basic and essential oils from plants all over the world are used in developing very faint scents that have an impact on the human body. The Japanese use it in many of their operations. Certain aromas induce high levels of energy which assist people in working at their peak performance. Others induce relaxation and calmness. These are subtly introduced into the ventilation systems to help people get through the day. Near the end of the day the scent is changed to help people relax before going home. Have you ever wondered why a glass of water with a thin slice of lemon is more refreshing than a plain glass of water?

Health The concept of total health is not new. Today it is sold as exercising equipment. The real marketing tool is a good looking body, thanks to an exercise machine and a special drink that makes you think you are achieving total health. It is impossible to separate the mind, body and spirit in achieving total health. Mental attitude is as important to total health as physical condition. Contentment, living in harmony with nature and the world around you are just as important.

From ancient times until today, the true basic formula has never changed. It requires that you

- Choose a proper diet (not loaded with synthetic materials the FDA says are fine)
- Exercise moderation in everything (alcohol, eating, exercise, etc.)
- Exercise our bodies (stretching, physical activity)
- Exercise our minds (meditation, reading, openness)
- Relax (massage, shiatsu, reflexology)
- Exercise our energy level of consciousness (believing in ourselves, giving freely to others)
- Eliminate destructive behavior (fear, dominance, territorialism)
- Extend empathy and compassion to others (hug someone, although in today's society you'll probably get sued)

There are no secrets, just a lack of understanding by individuals and organizations that it takes time for total health to develop.

Relaxation Try to sit still for 30 minutes. You can't. Why? There isn't time, and we don't know how. Think of how this affects our perception of the world. Think how this constant anxiety affects those around us. Think how this affects our health and state of mind. Relaxation is not becoming lazy, it's becoming balanced within your mind and body to achieve what is important to you the family, society and the organization.

Choice # 8 - Nature and the Environment

A critical consideration that can't be overlooked is the effect our lifestyle has on our environment, The fact is, nature will always seek to rebalance the equation—peacefully over time, or radically through natural disaster. Until this decade the human race has, to a large degree, been able to live in balance with nature. The shift to imbalance began in the 1800's and escalated exponentially through the 1900's. Today we are actively destroying our natural surroundings at an alarming rate to (allegedly) improve our standard of living and economic productivity. Many of us begrudge the government's interference in mandating environmental laws and regulations. The place to begin eliminating destructive practices is in ourselves.

Many ancient philosophers and civilizations have predicted this destruction and the results that will occur. The Hopi Prophecy (Native American) clearly outlines the final outcome of modern civilization if we continue down our current path. Many of the signs that were predicted have already occurred, indicating that little (if any) time remains to change to prevent natural rebalancing through widespread devastation. The Ogala Sioux (Native American) have a similar prophecy that refers to a "Blue Man" surrounded by dead and dying vegetation. Other civilizations and religions have similar prophecies, and each contains the opportunity for the human race to change its direction and avoid the natural catastrophic events. The book of Revelations in the Bible describes many of the same events, but the context is based more in fear than in opportunity for change. Most interesting is the fact that these prophecies were developed at different times, hundreds and sometimes thousands of years apart, by different cultures, by different religions and yet all come to the same general conclusion, including the time frame—within our current lifetime.

The resources and beauty offered to us through nature are ours to enjoy and preserve for future generations. Instead we are destroying. This century we have experienced major wars, earthquakes, flooding, volcanic activity, overpopulation, famine, killing drought, depletion of the ozone layer, depletion of the rain forests, the extinction of natural species, etc. Nature has also begun to surprise us with HIV, E-Bolla and other new creations that we are unprepared to handle. Is this nature's means of beginning to rebalance the effects of the overcrowded human species?

In order to take individual responsibility for rebalancing nature and our relationship with the environment, we must take a tough new look at our lifestyles. What are the true essentials? Are all the synthetic compounds really necessary? Can we become less materialistic? Isn't it worth paying more to purchase and recycle items from easily renewable resources (corn, beans, wheat, hemp, etc.) instead of destroying rain forests that will never be replaced in our grandchildren's lifetime? These options exist today for nearly everything that we purchase. But the options are rarely commercialized due to higher costs. The companies we all work for are using non-replenishable resources every day. This is not to say that every organization is bad or that basic human nature is bad. But we can't continue the destruction. We must focus on the alternatives regardless of costs and the change in our lifestyles. If we don't have the willpower to do it, the rebalancing force of nature will take care of the problem for us, but at a much higher price.

SUPPLEMENTAL GUIDE

The purpose of this section is to provide a way for you to test your sense of reality in the workplace and your view of yourself. It is intended as a guide to begin a thinking process that will help you prioritize the personal and professional changes that are needed. The information provides only a general sense of direction and is not, nor is it intended to be, detailed and all-inclusive.

The first segment is designed to let you review the meanings of certain phrases, and then compare your thoughts with those of the people you work with. The differences between perceptions are the gap areas which need to be addressed in order to begin focusing the organization on higher performance. Following each group of questions you should consider developing your own GAP chart to plan and measure the progress and quality of change.

Reviewing Your Current Business Situation

1. To me, *world class* means :

   My co-workers define world class as :

   The top three differences in perception are :

2. To me, *becoming the best* means :

   My co-workers define becoming the best as :

The top three differences in perception are :

3. To me, *intellectual capital* means :

   My co-workers define intellectual capital as :

   For me, the best way to secure intellectual capital is :

   My co-workers believe intellectual capital is best secured through :

   The top three differences to be addressed are :

4. The mission of my company (department or job) is to :

   My co-worker defines the mission of the company (department or job) as :

   The top three differences are :

With the answers to these simple questions you will begin to see a pattern that indicates whether the organization has a well defined and communicated mission that is clear to all employees. If the answers show a wide variation you need to go to square one and determine the root cause of the confusion and determine how you will deal with correcting the situation.

Reviewing the Perception of the Common Tools

4. To me, *downsizing* means :

   I believe that downsizing is (or is not) necessary because :

   My co-workers define downsizing as :

   My co-workers believe that downsizing is (is not) necessary because :

   The three primary issues that we must address are :

   The three primary complaints about downsizing are :

5. To me, *reengineering* means :

   My co-workers define reengineering as :

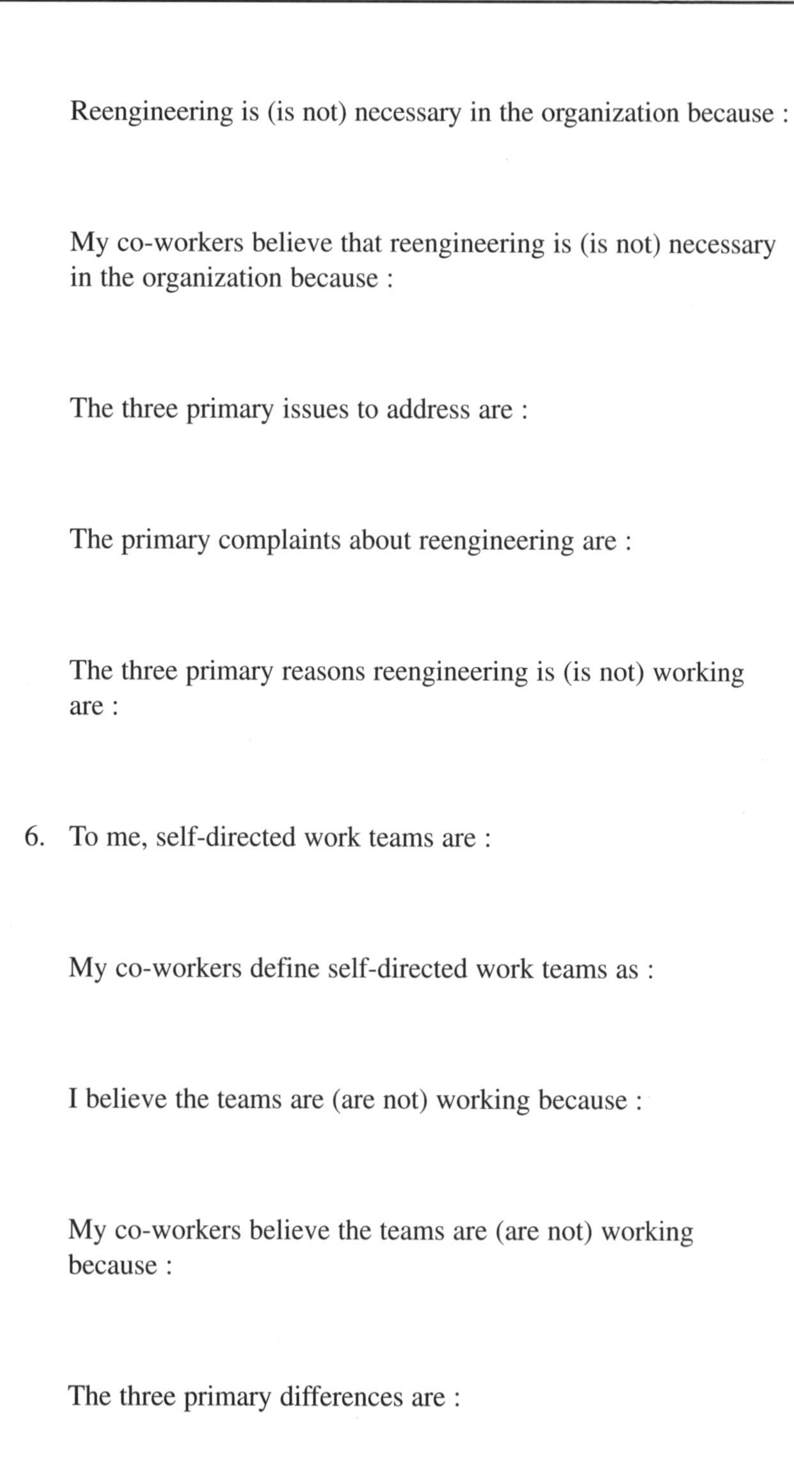

Reengineering is (is not) necessary in the organization because :

My co-workers believe that reengineering is (is not) necessary in the organization because :

The three primary issues to address are :

The primary complaints about reengineering are :

The three primary reasons reengineering is (is not) working are :

6. To me, self-directed work teams are :

My co-workers define self-directed work teams as :

I believe the teams are (are not) working because :

My co-workers believe the teams are (are not) working because :

The three primary differences are :

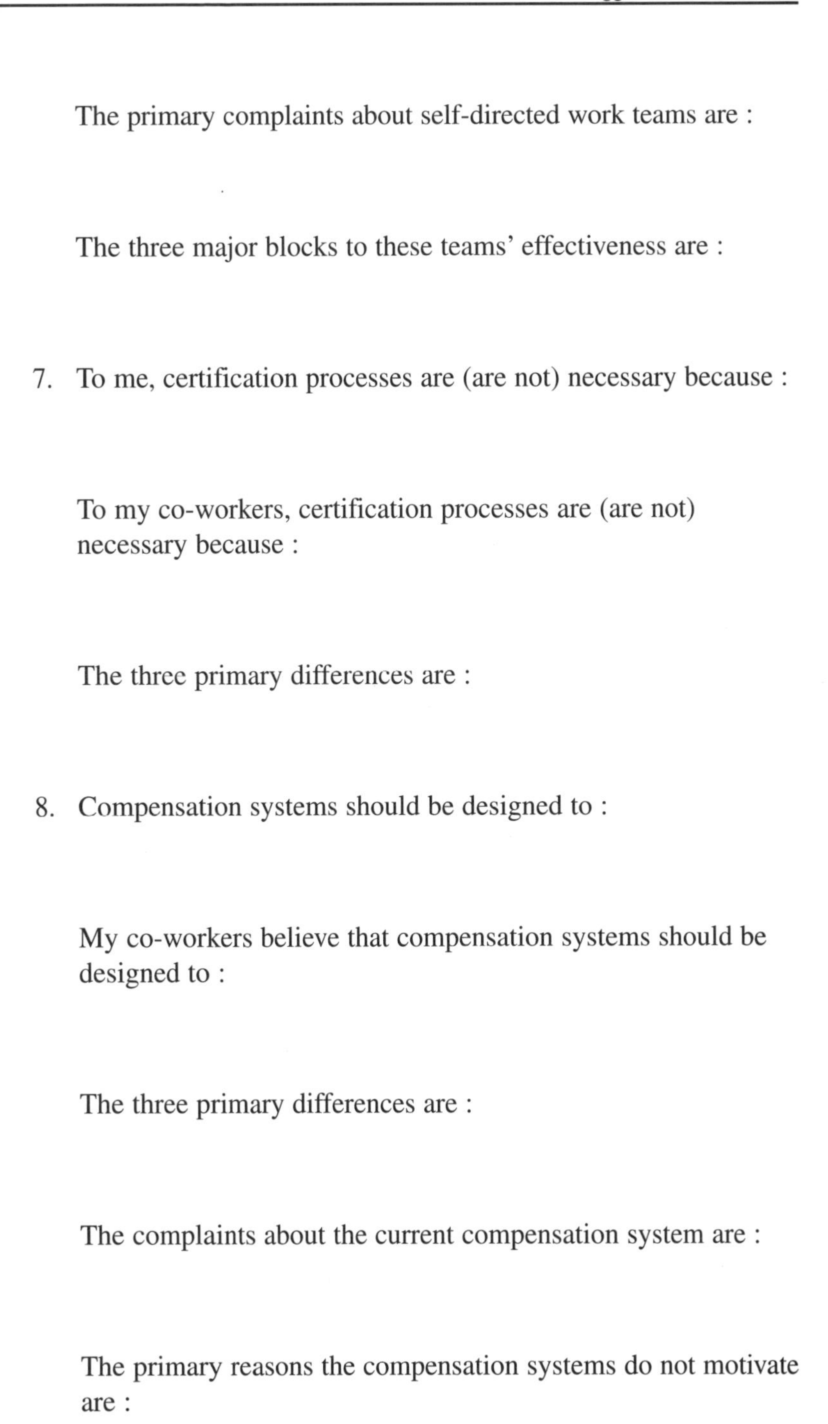

The primary complaints about self-directed work teams are :

The three major blocks to these teams' effectiveness are :

7. To me, certification processes are (are not) necessary because :

   To my co-workers, certification processes are (are not) necessary because :

   The three primary differences are :

8. Compensation systems should be designed to :

   My co-workers believe that compensation systems should be designed to :

   The three primary differences are :

   The complaints about the current compensation system are :

   The primary reasons the compensation systems do not motivate are :

9. I believe that consultants are (are not) necessary to :

   I believe that consultants should be used when :

   My co-workers believe that consultants are (are not) necessary because :

   My co-workers believe that consultants should be used when :

   The three primary differences are :

   The primary complaints about management's use of consultants are :

10. To me, empowerment means :

    To my co-workers empowerment means :

    The three primary areas to address are :

    The three major blocks to empowerment are :

11. To me, alternative work schedules :

    To my co-workers alternative work schedules :

    The road blocks to alternative work schedules are :

    The three primary areas to address are :

12. To me information systems are :

    and must include :

    To my co-workers, information systems are :

    and must include :

    The three differences in the perceived types and needs of information systems are :

    The three primary areas to address are :

The purpose of this section is demonstrate to you that your perceptions of the existing systems—their meaning, intent and effectiveness—are usually quite different than those held by others in your organization. You will begin to see patterns revealing differences in the perceptions of managers, clerks, production employees, research employees and sales employees. These differences are real and need to be addressed in order to bring the organization into focus.

What is the potential cause of our system failures?

13. The fears that exist within the organization are :

    and they exist due to :

    My co-workers believe that the fears that exist within the organization are :

    and they exist due to :

    The unwritten rules and sacred cows within the organization are :

    My co-workers believe the unwritten rules and sacred cows that exist are :

    The areas that need to be addressed in order to eliminate the unwritten rules and sacred cows are:

The three primary reasons for fear-based motivation in the organization that must be eliminated are :

14. The manner in which my ego contributes in a positive (or negative) manner to the organization is :

    My co-workers state that my ego helps (or blocks) :

    The areas that I must take responsibility (in myself) to improve are :

    The examples and resulting effects of ego within the organization are :

    The examples and resulting effects of ego behavior that my co-workers see are :

    To correct this we (I) must take responsibility to change :

15. The territorial and dominant behavior I observe within the organization is :

    The territorial and dominant behavior I observe within myself is :

The territorial and dominant behavior my co-workers observe within the organization and within my actions are :

These behaviors can be controlled or eliminated within the organization by :

In the opinion of my co-workers, these behaviors can be controlled or eliminated through :

The three primary changes we (I) must take responsibility for are :

In my personal life :

In my professional life :

In building relationships :

The purpose of the above section, although short, is to draw attention to the many barriers that each of us creates for ourselves and for others through non-productive energy and behaviors. Although some individuals may be able to address the changes on their own, most will need some guidance and assistance.

Value Systems

Take a moment to review the graphs and information regarding value systems. A detailed training session in this area is available as with the other sections. For simplistic purposes however, let's look at how the various value systems would answer the following question: "Why do I wear a tie to work?"

System 1	No response. Cannot comprehend the meaning.
System 2	Because the boss wears one.
System 3	I don't care if the boss does it or not, I'll wear whatever I want to wear and no one will tell me differently.
System 4	Because on page 57, paragraph 3, sub section (a), the rule book states that all managers will wear ties.
System 5	The boss wears one and in order to get the better jobs and more money I'll play along with the boss.
System 6	The group feels that is right given our jobs so we have all agreed that it is best for the group.
System 7	I wear one when it is appropriate and don't wear one when I don't believe that its appropriate.

Concentrate on the value systems graphs. This is the typical make-up of the managerial and non-managerial value systems within your business. These two graphs clearly identify how systems and processes fail if the difference value systems is not addressed. Recognizing these differences and structuring the programs accordingly will breathe new energy into the organization.

Is there tolerance and acceptance of differences?

16. To me, tolerance and acceptance mean :

    To my co-workers, tolerance and acceptance mean :

    Demonstration of tolerance and acceptance by me and within the organization have occurred when :

    Demonstration of tolerance and acceptance as perceived by my co-workers have occurred when :

    The three greatest barriers to full tolerance and acceptance in myself and the organization are :

    My co-workers consider the largest barriers to be :

    I/We can improve the tolerance and acceptance of differences by :

The purpose of the section above is to recognize that tolerance and acceptance are very important in developing the potential of the individual and the organization. Too often we hire people just like ourselves and tend to not accept those who are unlike ourselves. The elimination of this tendency will lead to greater potential.

Is there an understanding of basic personality traits?

Observe yourself and others when change is introduced into the comfort zones at work or at home. The language and the behavior are the key indicators of the type of personality that you are projecting to others, or are dealing with in others. What happens when change occurs? The first type of individual will become upset and rebellious, the second type will talk to many individuals to try and influence the outcome through changes to the initial change, the third type will continually question the change and may never get to a point of acceptance, the fourth type will become very stubborn until control can be established and the fifth type will respond as deemed appropriate given all the facts.

What type of behavior do you see in yourself and in others? To make the changes smoother, all of these traits must be considered and the appropriate responses and plans should be developed prior to an announcement.

Team Dynamics

17. How do you define a self-directed or self-disciplined work team?

    How do your co-workers define a self-directed or self-disciplined work team?

    What is the gap and how can it be closed?

Refer to the earlier discussion on team dynamics and the structuring of an effective team to review all the basic principles.

Communications

18. Effective communication to me means :

    Effective communications to my co-workers means :

    The three most significant differences :

    What changes can be implemented into the communication systems that will have the desired impact?

Refer back to the sections on both communication and value systems. Remember that some people accept only written communications and others accept only verbal communications. How do you best design a system for your organization that will meet everyone's needs and be continually current?

Defining the Best Organizational Structure

19. Do you believe that you have a process or specialized organizational structure?

    Do your co-workers believe that you have a process or specialized organizational structure?

What do you believe are the real impediments to organizational effectiveness?

What do your co-workers believe are the real impediments to organizational effectiveness?

The three primary changes that must take place are :

Review the sections regarding organizational structure, value systems and destructive personality types in formulating your decisions.

Benefits and Compensation

20. Compensation and benefit systems which are fair, equitable and motivating incorporate :

    My co-workers believe that compensation and benefit programs which are fair, equitable and motivating incoporate :

    What are the three most prominent problems that surface and how can you change these problems?

Remember that the workforce and our society are changing and the desires of the past are no longer valid for future employees. Refer to the sections on benefits and compensation, and striking a balance in life.

Striking a Balance in Life

21. Happiness with balance between your personal and professional life means :

    Is your family happy with the balance?

    My co-workers define happiness with the balance between their personal and professional lives as :

    What do they tell you their families believe?

    What are the three major differences?

    How can these differences be rectified?

Remember that the workforce and society are changing. Those who are truly satisfied are quite often those who have the most balance in their lives, and have driven out fear and lack of identity.

THE INTEGRATED PRODUCTIVITY CENTER

The Center for Integrated Productivity is an independent consulting consortium operating in conjunction with other consulting firms. The purpose of the Center is to offer a new way of focusing on the business environment to achieve and maintain high performance without the personal and environmental costs that so often are part of success. The Center is dedicated to the development of a balanced approach to winning strategies that benefit corporations, people, communities and the environment. The Center offers workshops on numerous topics within this book and provides on-site consulting services. If you would like more information on the workshops and services available, please write to:

The Center for Integrated Productivity
P.O. Box 424
Marion, IA. 52302
Ph. 319-377-0001
Fax 319-377-0001
E-mail: Comupserve 103105.467